Give Up
Worry
for Lent!

"Gary Zimak is someone who is not afraid to tell people that the only way to find lasting peace is by getting close to Jesus. In *Give Up Worry for Lent!* Zimak guides the reader—step by step—to cultivate a habit of trust in the Lord that will help them celebrate Easter with newfound joy."

Fr. Jeffrey Kirby
Author of *Be Not Troubled*

"Lent is a time of opportunity: to claim the peace that Christ won for us upon the Cross. Occasionally we come across a practical resource that helps us take full advantage of this opportunity. Gary Zimak's book does this beautifully. I encourage you to get your hands on the book and journey toward finding peace in Christ."

Fr. Rob Galea
Author of *Breakthrough*

"This wonderfully engaging and inspiring book will move your heart in a powerful way. If you are battling worry or anxiety, pick up a copy of this book as part of your Lenten journey and watch your faith come alive!"

Deacon Harold Burke-Sivers
Author of *Behold the Man*

"Finally, I can give up something for Lent that will have profound and lasting effects on my spiritual/daily life. I can't wait to shed the worrying using Zimak's scripture-based method for the forty-day journey. This is definitely my Lenten book of choice!"

Debbie Georgianni
Cohost of EWTN's *Take 2 with Jerry and Debbie*

"With candor, clarity, and compassion, Gary Zimak offers us all a way to 'make all things new' for Lent. If you need a spiritual faith lift, pick up a copy of this little book and read it, pray with it, and share it. It will change the way you approach Easter—and might even change your life."

Deacon Greg Kandra
Blogger at *The Deacon's Bench*

"*Give Up Worry for Lent!* is one of the most important Lenten books you'll ever read. Gary Zimak adeptly confronts one of the most prevalent spiritual obstacles of our time—worry—and equips us to confront it for ourselves. He weaves together Scripture, personal anecdotes, Church wisdom, and prayer with finesse. Meaty, meaningful, and mighty!"

Marge Fenelon
Author of *Our Lady, Undoer of Knots*

"Before reading a book, I first look to see whether the messenger's life gives him the street cred to deliver such a message. Zimak and his family have already embraced the overcoming life adventure that this book challenges and equips us to live. They walk this walk. Take this book with you this Lenten season as your adventure guide."

Bear Woznick
Founder of Deep Adventure Ministries

Give Up Worry for Lent!

40 DAYS TO FINDING PEACE IN CHRIST

GARY ZIMAK

AᴠE Mᴀʀɪᴀ Pʀᴇss AVE Notre Dame, Indiana

Contents

"THE END"

The End? Wait, shouldn't this be the introduction?

If you find this a bit confusing, let me explain why I think "The End" is the perfect title for the introduction of this book . . . after I make a few points.

Over the years, I have given up many things for Lent, and I'll bet you have, too. But how many of those things have changed your life and brought you closer to God? My guess would be not too many. One of my favorite Lenten sacrifices was giving up sweets, but I spent more time during those forty days dreaming about cakes and candy than I did thinking about the Lord. And when Easter Sunday rolled around, I gorged myself with multiple sweets and continued to do so throughout the year. For me, Lent did not produce a positive, permanent spiritual change.

What is Lent all about? The first recorded words of Jesus in Mark's gospel sum it up nicely: "The time is fulfilled, and the kingdom of God is at hand; repent, and believe in the gospel" (Mk 1:15).

Since the gospels were originally written in Greek, looking at the original manuscript can be very helpful for understanding the meaning more fully. The Greek word used for "repent" is *metanoia*, which implies a spiritual change of heart. Lent is a time to turn away from our earthly attachments and turn toward Christ. Therefore, our Lenten practices should in some way help us to achieve that goal.

While giving up sweets, alcohol, or social media for Lent can certainly be offered up as suffering and used by the Lord, it is debatable whether forgoing them will bring about a lasting change in our lives. Giving up sweets for almost seven weeks didn't help me in the long run and will probably not help you either. What can we do?

WORRY: THE BAD HABIT IT FEELS GOOD TO GIVE UP

There are many vices or bad habits that keep us from growing closer to God, but there is one that hits close to home for me—worry. It is no secret that I have struggled with anxiety for most of my life. I have written several books and appeared all over Catholic media telling the story of my struggles with worry. It started when I was about six years old and wreaked havoc with my life for decades. Panic attacks, heart palpitations, digestive problems—I've had them all! It wasn't until I met Jesus Christ and turned my life over to him that I was able to find peace. I can assure you that life without worry is possible, but you can't do it by yourself.

"I want you to be free from anxieties" (1 Cor 7:32). These words were written by St. Paul through the inspiration of the Holy Spirit. Therefore, his words convey a message directly from God. If God wants us to be free from anxieties, it must be possible to stop worrying! I am living proof that it is possible. If I can stop worrying, you can too.

You hold in your hands a one-day-at-a-time method for banishing worry from your life. More importantly, the exercises in this book will also help you draw closer to the Lord, entering into a deeper relationship with him. Each daily exercise consists of a Bible verse, a brief meditation, a call to action, and a prayer. While not necessarily taken from the daily Mass readings, these verses follow the rhythm of the Lenten season.

You will also see that I've included readings for the Sundays of Lent (so there are forty-seven readings, rather than forty). The reason for this is simple: Technically, Lenten Sundays are not days of fasting and abstinence, but I want to make sure you have something to read every day during Lent. So I've included forty-*seven* readings so you will have something to read each day from Ash Wednesday through Holy Week and right into Easter! (Wasn't that nice of me?)

WHY DID I WRITE THIS BOOK?

There are a few things you should know about me before we start. I am not a therapist, counselor, or psychologist, and I cannot offer professional advice on overcoming anxiety. What I can offer you, however, is the story of how Jesus Christ transformed my life. With his help, I am more peaceful than ever before. And that's what I want to share with you—how Jesus helped me overcome the worry habit.

What have you got to lose? Try these daily devotions during this Lenten season and see what happens. Even if I don't know you personally, I know the Lord. Once you are in contact with him, great things will happen.

Remember the title of the introduction? The journey that you are about to take involves closing the door on the past. Every new beginning is preceded by an ending. You are invited to end your old life of worrying and enter into a new life of peace, with Jesus as your guide. My prayer is that you will continue to enjoy the peace of Christ—not just during this Lenten season but for the rest of your life.

Let's get started!

Days 1-4

WEEK OF ASH WEDNESDAY

THOUGHT FOR THE WEEK

Yesterday is gone, tomorrow has not yet come. We have only today. Let us begin.
—St. Teresa of Calcutta[1]

Day 1

TIME TO REST

Ash Wednesday

READ

> Come to me, all who labor and are heavy
> laden, and I will give you rest.
>
> —Matthew 11:28

REFLECT

As you begin this Lenten journey, reflect on an offer from Jesus that is too good to pass up. It doesn't matter what is weighing you down or causing you to worry, the promise is the same—rest.

I remember hanging on to this verse during a very difficult time in my life. My wife was pregnant with our twin daughters, and the girls were not expected to live. In fact, they only had a 10 percent chance of being born alive. We had just left the perinatal clinic at Our Lady of Lourdes Hospital in Camden, New Jersey. An ultrasound had revealed that Mary and Elizabeth were still alive—although the prognosis remained grim.

We paid a visit to the hospital chapel and knelt before Jesus in the tabernacle. My eyes drifted to the writing above the sanctuary, and I saw the Bible verse at the top of this reflection. If there was ever a time I felt heavy laden, this was it. I accepted the Lord's offer and imagined myself running toward him. Immediately, I felt the comfort he promised. I didn't know how things would turn out (miraculously, the girls did survive), but for the moment, I was at peace.

It doesn't matter how many Lents you have wasted in the past. Begin anew today. It is the first day of a brand-new Lent. Are you ready to depart from habitual worrying and follow him? He doesn't promise a problem-free life, and he doesn't guarantee that you won't suffer. What he promises is something only he can give—peace. Not a worldly peace that ebbs and flows with your circumstances but a supernatural peace that can't be taken away by the problems of life.

At this point, let's not focus on how impossible it seems not to worry or how many times peace has eluded you in the past. Instead, concentrate on his words. Don't you desire to accept his offer? It's very attractive, isn't it?

Now, here's the catch. While the Lord's offer is extended to all, you and I are free to reject it. Why would anyone do that? There could be any number of reasons, including that we don't trust him or it seems too good to be true.

How about if you let this Lent be different than those in the past? Read and reread the invitation from Jesus. There are no caveats or qualifications. If you come to him, you will find rest. Period. Are you willing to give it a try?

RESPOND

Make the decision to run to Jesus and accept his invitation. Tell him you are willing to trust him (even if you don't feel like it) and desperately desire the peace that he offers. Let that be your Lenten goal.

PRAY

Jesus, I am burdened with many worries. Although it seems impossible, I want to experience the rest that you promise. My goal this Lent is to follow you more closely. Instead of trying to stop worrying all by myself, I will focus on following you. Thank you, Lord. I am hopeful. Amen.

Day 2

FOCUS ON THE LORD

Thursday after Ash Wednesday

READ

Set your minds on things that are above, not
on things that are on earth.

—Colossians 3:2

REFLECT

Today is the second day of Lent, and it's time to look at the
first step in eliminating worry from your life. The answer is
as simple as what St. Paul tells the people of Colossae in the
above verse. You need to think about God more than you
think about your problems. If you constantly dwell on your
earthly challenges and difficulties, you will never experience
peace in your life. If, on the other hand, you keep your focus
on the Lord and turn to him each day, you will be at peace.

This does not mean that you should ignore the problems
in your life. It means that you should let God help you to
handle them. Most of us who are anxious by nature like to
be in control. When we face a situation that is beyond our
control, we often begin to worry. How can we overcome this?
We begin by recognizing that the Lord, who truly is in control,
wants to be part of our lives. He doesn't expect us to handle

the challenges of life alone. Rather, he wants us to do what we can and ask for his assistance with the heavy lifting.

Over the course of the next several weeks, we are going to work on doing this one day at a time. For now, let's focus on the fact that there is a bigger picture than just this life and its problems. Lent provides us the opportunity to look upward and remember that we were created to live with God forever in heaven. Before we get there, however, there is suffering to contend with on earth. As Catholics, we believe that this suffering has value and can help us (and those around us) reach our final goal of eternal happiness.

While it's impossible to stop yourself from being afraid, it is possible to turn your thoughts to God. Your brain cannot process two thoughts at the same time. Every minute spent thinking about the Lord (or better yet, conversing with him) is one less minute spent thinking about your problems. There are only twenty-four hours in a day. Your ultimate goal should be more "God time" than "worrying time." It will take work at first, but it will be worth it.

RESPOND

While it sounds easy to spend time thinking about God instead of your problems, it can be difficult without setting concrete goals. Today, read the words of Jesus in John 14:1–3 and spend ten minutes picturing what heaven will be like. Ask the Holy Spirit to guide your thoughts.

PRAY

Heavenly Father, thank you for preparing a room in heaven just for me. You created me so that I could enter into a relationship with you. Even though I tend to get sidetracked by dwelling on my problems, I want to change. Please grant me the desire to focus on you instead of my earthly difficulties. Amen.

Day 3

OPEN YOUR DOOR FOR JESUS

Friday after Ash Wednesday

READ

> Lift up your heads, O gates!
>> and be lifted up, O ancient doors!
>> that the King of glory may come in.
>> —Psalm 24:7

REFLECT

One of my favorite paintings is *Christ at Heart's Door* by Warner Sallman. It depicts Jesus knocking on the front door of a house. What makes the image particularly striking is the fact that there is no doorknob on the outside of the door. As a result, it can only be opened from the inside. As unusual as this is, it accurately represents how Jesus approaches us. Instead of forcing his way into our lives, he gently knocks on the door of our hearts and waits for us to open it and invite him inside.

The decision to open the door is one that only you can make. Although he wants to be a part of your life, Jesus will not force open the door. Make no mistake about it, however: he will knock and knock again. Before you wonder why he never seems to knock on your door, let me pass along one other piece of information. It is especially important if you're a worrier. Every time you are afraid, Jesus *is* knocking on your door.

What are the things that are frightening you at this time? Sickness? Job loss? An uncertain future? All of these things (and many more) are ways in which Jesus knocks on your door. When this happens, you have two choices: you can turn inward and worry, or you can open the door and let him in.

Can it really be that simple? Absolutely. But just because it's simple doesn't mean that it's easy. We are so used to worrying about our problems that this thought seems downright unrealistic. That's what I used to think until I tried it. When you invite Jesus Christ to enter your life and help you with your problems, he will not refuse. Are you ready to open the door?

RESPOND

What occupies more time in your life—worrying or praying? It has been my experience that the vast majority of Christians often forget about the Lord when problems arise. Sure, we remember to send up some prayers, but then we lapse into the useless practice of worrying. That will change for you today when you pray the following prayer. It's not a magic formula, a trite expression, or a self-help mantra. Rather, it is a very real invitation to a very real person who will change your life if you let him.

PRAY

Dear Jesus, I hear you knocking on my door and I am ready to let you into my life. Please be patient with me, as this is all very new. I'm not used to trusting you with my problems, but I'm ready to give it a try. I turn my worries over to you and ask you to handle them for me. Thank you. Amen.

Day 4

GIVE HIM YOUR PROBLEMS

Saturday after Ash Wednesday

READ

> Jesus Christ is the same yesterday and today
> and for ever.
>
> —Hebrews 13:8

REFLECT

Just for a minute, picture what it would be like if Jesus walked into the room right now. Standing before you, he asks you the same question that he asked the blind beggar Bartimaeus prior to healing him: "What do you want me to do for you?" (Mk 10:51). If you're anything like me, there are several requests that would immediately come to mind. How often do you take him up on his offer and ask him for what you need?

I'm not going to kid you and say that it's easy to picture Jesus at all times, because it isn't. But I am going to point out what the Bible tells us—Jesus Christ is every bit as real today as he was when he walked the face of the earth two thousand years ago. Keeping that fact in mind is critical if you want to experience peace in this life. Even more important is acting on the belief that he is alive and present—even if it doesn't feel like it.

One of my favorite Bible stories is the journey of the two disciples to Emmaus (see Luke 24:13–35). As the story unfolds, we learn that the travelers are saddened by the crucifixion of Jesus, having "hoped that he was the one to redeem Israel." While their grief seems reasonable, given what just happened, they are missing a key point: the risen Jesus is walking with them. He is not dead and did indeed redeem Israel, just as he promised. These men should have been ecstatic, but instead they are sad. Why? Because they didn't recognize the presence of Jesus in their lives. And so they struggled on, carrying their burdens alone—and so unnecessarily!

The same Jesus who walked with these disciples is with you today and ready to perform miracles in your life. The fact that you don't feel his presence doesn't change anything. He is with you. You can't see or feel electricity, but you express your belief in it every time you flip a light switch. Do the same thing with Jesus today. Put aside the thoughts that he doesn't feel real to you.

RESPOND

Yesterday you opened the door and welcomed Jesus into your life. Today it's time to give him your problems. Even if they seem like mountains to you, they are no big deal for him. He healed the sick, gave sight to the blind, and rose from the dead. He can find you a job, cure your illness, guide your children back to church, or restore your hope. Ask him, even if it doesn't seem like he's really there. By the way, if you're worried that you might forget about him, get into the habit of saying "Jesus" every time you turn on the lights. It may sound simple, but it's a great reminder!

PRAY

Jesus, thank you for your constant presence in my life. I know that you care about me. I am concerned about (*list your top fears*). They seem like big issues to me, but I know they are no big deal for you. Please help me! Amen.

Days 5–11

FIRST WEEK
OF LENT

THOUGHT FOR THE WEEK

Nothing is more destined to create deep-seated anxieties in people than the false assumption that life should be free from anxieties.

—Ven. Fulton J. Sheen[2]

Day 5

BEWARE YOUR ENEMY'S TRICKS

First Sunday of Lent

READ

> Be sober, be watchful. Your adversary the
> devil prowls around like a roaring lion, seek-
> ing some one to devour.
>
> —1 Peter 5:8

REFLECT

In today's gospel reading, as well as in the first letter of Peter, quoted above, we learn a valuable lesson about Satan—he is extremely confident and persistent. And while I don't want to give him too much credit, we do need to take him seriously. If he had the audacity to tempt Jesus, don't think for a minute that he won't try to tempt you too. He will. Unfortunately for us, he is very good at what he does. Trying to get us to turn away from God, he strikes where we are weakest.

Satan has many different tricks up his sleeve, but he often tempts those of us who are anxious in the same way—by playing into our fears. He wants us to worry. Why? Because whenever we worry, we are moving away from God and focusing on ourselves. That makes the evil one very happy. We'll get into the difference between fear and worry in the days to come, but just be aware that they are two different things. Fear is an emotion and is morally neutral. Worry is an action and can be controlled.

Even though Satan can be very sneaky, there is no need to panic. He can't *make* you do anything, though he will use all kinds of tricks and tactics to get you to worry. According to the *Catechism of the Catholic Church*, "The power of Satan is, nonetheless, not infinite. He is only a creature, powerful from the fact that he is pure spirit, but still a creature. He cannot prevent the building up of God's reign" (395).

He can lie to you, he can tempt you, but Satan can't make you turn away from God and commit a sin. He does not have power over you. Know that he's going to pester you, know that he rejoices when you worry, but always remember the words of Jesus and get into the habit of using them: "Get behind me, Satan!" (Mt 16:23).

RESPOND

Sometimes Satan is responsible for your worrying. (And sometimes he isn't.) Regardless of his role in it, the evil one is ecstatic whenever you do succumb to worry. It may sound overly simplistic, but a good spiritual rule of thumb is to avoid doing anything that makes Satan happy. The following prayer invokes the intercession of St. Michael the Archangel and is a good one to pray every day. It will help.

PRAY

St. Michael the Archangel, defend us in battle. Be our defense against the wickedness and snares of the devil. May God rebuke him, we humbly pray, and do thou, O Prince of the heavenly hosts, by the power of God, thrust into hell Satan and all the evil spirits, who prowl about the world seeking the ruin of souls. Amen.

Day 6

YES, GOD CAN HANDLE IT

Monday—First Week of Lent

READ

> For with God nothing will be impossible.
> —Luke 1:37

REFLECT

There is a tendency for many Christians (and non-Christians) to underestimate the power of God. Much of it has to do with the limitations of our human intellect, but some of it is due to cynicism. Our lips may proclaim that he can do all things, but our hearts just can't buy it. If it's impossible, then it can't happen. Before we go any further, we need to address this head on. With God, *nothing* is impossible.

Let's look at the statement a little closer. These words were spoken to the Blessed Mother by the archangel Gabriel, after he relayed the news that she was chosen to be the mother of the long-awaited Messiah. After giving her the basic details and answering her one and only question—"How can this be, since I have no husband?" (Lk 1:34)—Gabriel informed Mary that Elizabeth (her elderly and childless cousin) was six months pregnant. He then concluded with the message that nothing will be impossible for God.

While it's possible that Gabriel was providing that last piece of information as evidence to help sway Mary's decision, I have come to believe that this message was designed more for future generations. Mary's faith was undoubtedly strong enough to say yes to God's plan, but my faith is not. I need to hear this message, and I'm very glad that the Holy Spirit inspired St. Luke to include it in the narrative.

Putting aside God's logic for giving Gabriel those words, it's easy to see that the virgin birth (and the Word becoming flesh) is a great example of God's omnipotent power. But here's something to consider. Does the concept of the virgin birth help you to believe that nothing is impossible for God? Is that occurrence enough for you to face a cancer diagnosis, extended unemployment, or infertility and say, "No problem, Lord. I know you can handle this"? How about the fact that Jesus died and rose from the dead? Is that sufficient?

As a Catholic, I believe wholeheartedly that both of these events took place and are great examples of God's infinite power. Unfortunately, this knowledge doesn't always prevent me from panicking when a crisis appears in my life. How can I make myself believe in my heart that God can truly do all things? I can't, but God can.

RESPOND

As we read the words of Gabriel today, we are reminded of the fact that God can fix any problem that we will ever face. For now, let's not dwell on "Why didn't he?" or "Why isn't he responding?" Instead let's concentrate on the fact that he can.

What can you do if you don't feel it? Ask him for help and expect him to respond.

PRAY

Heavenly Father, by faith I believe that you can do all things. I know it in my head but struggle to feel it in my heart. Please help me to believe that nothing is impossible for you. Amen.

Day 7

"WHAT IF . . . ?" GOD KNOWS

Tuesday—First Week of Lent

READ

> For I know the plans I have for you, says the
> LORD, plans for welfare and not for evil, to
> give you a future and a hope.
>
> —Jeremiah 29:11

REFLECT

Isn't this a great verse? You don't have to look very hard to find it on Christian plaques and inspirational websites. One of the reasons I love this message (it's even printed in bold letters on my Bible cover) is that it reminds me that even though I don't know what will happen in the future, God does. More importantly, these inspired words help me to remember that he is always in control.

I have worried about many things over the years, but the vast majority of my worries can be summed up by a two-word question: *What if?* And, even though I never kept score, I can state with absolute certainty that most of these potentially catastrophic problems either never took place or turned out much better than I expected. That still didn't stop me from wasting hundreds of hours playing the "What if?" game. Even sadder than the wasted time is the fact that there was someone with me who knew that I was suffering needlessly. That's right—God knew all along that I was worrying for no reason and would have been happy to help if I turned to him.

This message from the prophet Jeremiah was originally delivered to those who were taken from Jerusalem to Babylon and were living in exile. When Jeremiah first delivered this message to the people, things weren't looking too good for them. In his compassionate love, however, the Lord wanted to let them know that better days were ahead. It would take seventy years, but their suffering would end.

God is delivering the same message to you today. Sure, things may look bleak at the moment. The problems you are facing may seen unsolvable. Your suffering may be so intense that you don't know how you can endure another day. I've been there, and I know what you are going through. I have faced many hopeless problems, some real and some imaginary, in my life. And, while I didn't know how any of them would turn out, God always knew exactly what would happen.

One final thought to consider: In the above passage, the Lord acknowledges the plans that give you "a future and a hope." He wants you to live with him forever in heaven. Everything that happens in your life is designed to help make his plan a reality.

RESPOND

Most young children don't worry about the future. They typically live for the present moment and let their parents handle the "big stuff." Mom and Dad know that bills have to be paid and meals need to be prepared. Kids don't care, and rightfully so. We have a heavenly Father who is really good at handling the future. Let's allow him to do his job.

PRAY

Dear Father in heaven, my fear of the uncertainty of the future often causes me to plunge into excessive worry. Whenever I do that, I lose sight of your endless love and infinite power. Please help me to remember that it's your job to handle the future, and my job to live in the present moment. Amen.

Day 8

MOTHER KNOWS BEST

Wednesday—First Week of Lent

READ

> When the wine failed, the mother of Jesus
> said to him, "They have no wine."
>
> —John 2:3

REFLECT

Let's examine some of the important details contained in the story of the wedding at Cana (see John 2:1–11). The first thing to note is the order St. John lists the guests—Mary, Jesus, and the disciples. It seems obvious that the evangelist wants to call our attention to the mother of Jesus. She is there for a reason, and he wants to ensure that we don't miss that important detail. Next, we learn that the wine has run out. This would have been a big problem at a wedding feast in the day of our Lord, and it would be a big problem if it happened today. The people at the wedding are lacking something essential. They have a need that they can't satisfy themselves.

The only person who can fix the immediate problem is Jesus, and Mary knows it. As a result, she brings the problem to his attention. She doesn't tell him what to do or how to do it. All she does is let him know of the need: that there is no more wine. Jesus responds by turning water into wine, thus sparing the bride and groom from potential embarrassment. In addition to saving the wedding feast, this miracle (his first) causes the disciples to believe in him (see John 2:11).

Did Mary really need to tell Jesus about the wine situation? No. Because of his divine nature, he likely knew that the wine had run out. So why didn't he just take care of it? In all likelihood, he was waiting for his mother to ask. This is the first instance in the Bible where Mary turned to her Son and requested his help. Her intercession resulted in Jesus performing his first miracle.

Don't let yourself be confused by Jesus' initial response: "O woman, what have you to do with me?" Focus instead on her response to the servants: "Do whatever he tells you" (Jn 2:4, 5). The end result of Mary's intercession is that Jesus stepped in and saved the day.

The folks at the wedding lacked wine. What is your greatest need? Peace, health, money, greater love of neighbor, a better relationship with Jesus? Mary is ready to get involved and bring your intentions to Jesus. Will you let her?

RESPOND

You have an advantage over the guests at the wedding in Cana. Jesus had not yet performed any miracles so nobody (besides Mary) thought to turn to him for help. The idea of appealing to Mary would have been even more farfetched. The fact that this incident is documented in the Bible is a game changer. Mary's intercessory power is clearly evident. Make the decision to turn to her and ask her to accompany you on your Lenten journey, confident that she will take all of your petitions directly to Jesus.

PRAY

Hail Mary, full of grace,
the Lord is with thee.
Blessed art thou among women
and blessed is the fruit of thy womb, Jesus.
Holy Mary, Mother of God,
pray for us sinners now,
and at the hour of our death. Amen.

Day 9

SEEK CONTENTMENT

Thursday—First Week of Lent

READ

> I have learned, in whatever I am, to be content.
>
> —Philippians 4:11

REFLECT

I don't like fasting, especially from food. The mere mention of the word makes me cringe. Unfortunately, there's no getting around this traditional Catholic spiritual discipline. Without some form of fasting during Lent, our spiritual growth will be limited.

During this forty-day period given to us by the Church, we are urged to recognize that material comfort often keeps us from growing closer to Jesus. We are further called to forgo some of these earthly pleasures and focus on our relationship with the Lord. In doing so, we'll begin to understand what St. Paul means when he speaks of contentment.

Few of us would admit that we worship false gods, but how often do we turn to creature comforts, rather than to God, in times of fear or stress? Do you turn to God in prayer or do you eat, shop, or worry? While it's not something most of us consider, seeking comfort in earthly pleasures instead of God is essentially idol worship.

Now, don't panic. We all do this from time to time, and that's one of the reasons that the Church recommends fasting as an essential Lenten practice. In addition to giving us the opportunity to offer up our sufferings as a kind of penance, and strengthening our resolve against fleshly desires through self-denial (see *CCC*, 1438), going without helps us to realize just how much "stuff" means to us. Ultimately, only God can provide the lasting happiness that we all seek. It is an important lesson to learn.

In his letter to the Philippians, St. Paul discusses being content with what he has and rejoicing because the Lord is at hand. Pretty impressive for someone who was sitting in a Roman prison, don't you think? Try to imagine being content with what you have under those circumstances. Even more difficult to imagine is the ability to rejoice while being chained to a guard around the clock. Nothing could disturb Paul's peace.

That same kind of relationship with Jesus (and the peace that follows) is possible for each of us. It may take us many years (even a lifetime) to get anywhere close to that point, but that's what a relationship with Jesus can do.

RESPOND

Is your happiness based on external circumstances? Do you wish you could be more like St. Paul and learn to rejoice even when things aren't going your way? Lent provides the perfect opportunity to work on this very common problem. Spend some time today slowly reading and meditating on Psalm 100. This psalm serves as a reminder of what really matters. Pray for the guidance of the Holy Spirit before you begin. Ask him to point out the unique message that he has for you.

PSALM 100

Make a joyful noise to the LORD, all the lands!
> Serve the LORD with gladness!
> Come into his presence with singing!

Know that the LORD is God!
> It is he that made us, and we are his;
> we are his people, and the sheep of his pasture.

Enter his gates with thanksgiving,
> and his courts with praise!
> Give thanks to him, bless his name!

For the LORD is good;
> his steadfast love endures for ever,
> and his faithfulness to all generations.

PRAY

Dear Lord, help me to be content in all circumstances. By myself I cannot do this, but with your help I know I can feel your supernatural peace, no matter what is taking place around me. Amen.

Day 10

HELP OTHERS TO SEE JESUS

Friday—First Week of Lent

READ

> He must increase, but I must decrease.
> —John 3:30

REFLECT

If you're looking for a motto for your Lenten journey, these famous words from John the Baptist certainly do the trick. Following his advice will not only allow you to imitate Christ but also enable you to experience the peace that surpasses all understanding. There is one catch, however. In order to let Christ into your life, you must free up some room for him.

John knew what his role was to be and made it very clear to his followers that he was not the Messiah. Rather, John was the one chosen to announce the coming of the long-awaited Savior. In one sense, he seemed like a colossal failure in that he lost all of his followers to Jesus. When you look at the bigger picture, however, that is precisely what was supposed to happen. In order for the kingdom of God to grow, the role of John the Baptist had to decrease. Otherwise, he would have kept his followers away from Jesus instead of leading them to him.

When my family and I downsized and moved into a much smaller home last year, it caused us to make some difficult choices. It hit me especially hard when I realized that we had room for just one of my three bookcases. After spending much time determining which books would be kept, I ended up with one bookcase packed solid with the books that meant the most to me. What happens when I find a new must-have book? I have to free up room. Our spiritual lives operate in very much the same manner. If we want to grow close to Christ, we must make room for him.

Getting to know Jesus requires spending time with him. It is impossible to have a good relationship with him without spending daily time in prayer and spiritual reading. There is no shortcut. If you are reading this book, I would be willing to bet that you are looking for peace. Nothing I can say will give you that peace. Like John the Baptist, my goal is to send you to Jesus. He can and will provide the peace that you seek, but only if you spend time with him.

There are twenty-four hours in each day. If you sleep for eight hours, you have sixteen hours remaining. How much of that time do you spend on entertaining yourself, and how much time do you give the Lord? We all fall short in this category. Let's change that today.

RESPOND

Are you willing to give Jesus some of your "me" time today? I suggest that you start with ten minutes. Don't use family time or time that you are on the job. Instead, give Jesus ten minutes from your social media, television, or radio time. Converse with him in prayer or spend time reading the Bible. You may even want to consider doing this for the remainder of Lent. I guarantee it will be time well spent.

PRAY

Jesus, I want to know you better and look forward to spending some time with you today. Please increase my desire to grow close to you. Amen.

Day 11

FEAST UPON HIS WORD

Saturday—First Week of Lent

READ

> Your words were found, and I ate them,
> and your words became to me a joy and the
> delight of my heart.
>
> —Jeremiah 15:16

REFLECT

How often does God speak to you? Before you answer, I'd like to share what the Church teaches about this in the Vatican II document *Dei Verbum*:

> For in the sacred books, the Father who is in heaven meets His children with great love and speaks with them; and the force and power in the word of God is so great that it stands as the support and energy of the Church, the strength of faith for her sons, the food of the soul, the pure and everlasting source of spiritual life. [3]

Despite the fact that you may feel otherwise, God really does speak to you through the Bible. And, while it's not the only way he speaks, it is a very reliable method. Unlike your thoughts and feelings (which may or may not be from God), the Church affirms that the words found in sacred scripture are guaranteed to be inspired by God.

Of course, in the interest of full disclosure, I have to tell you that it is possible for God *not* to speak to you in the Bible. How? If you don't read it!

As a cradle Catholic, I can attest to the fact that many Catholics are not used to reading the Bible. If you fall into that category, however, don't worry—you can change! Furthermore, you don't need a theology degree to hear God speak to you through the Bible. You also don't need to understand everything that you read. What you need to understand is that the Lord can and will speak to you through sacred scripture.

If you need further reassurance, I encourage you to look back over the past ten meditations that we've covered. You have read at least one Bible verse every day. Were you aware that the Lord was speaking to you through those verses? You may not have realized it at the time, but that doesn't change things one bit. Every word in the Bible was inspired by God. When we read scripture, he is speaking to us. If it sounds simple, that's because it is.

For many years, I ignored God's voice in sacred scripture. I thought it was too difficult to understand and that it wouldn't make a big difference in my life. I was wrong. Like Jeremiah, I now understand that God's words in the Bible bring me great joy. When I'm having a bad day and feel the temptation to worry, opening his book brings me comfort. It may take some time and a little practice, but his words will comfort you too—but only if you read them.

Open it up, and feast upon his Word. Let him speak to you today.

RESPOND

As I mentioned earlier, you have already been reading the Bible each day and that's a good thing. We'll continue to do that for the remainder of Lent. For today, let's go back and review the statement from *Dei Verbum*, 21. Don't rush through it. Let the words sink in. It's an awesome message.

> For in the sacred books, the Father who is in heaven meets His children with great love and speaks with them; and the force and power in the word of God is so great that it stands as the support and energy of the Church, the strength of faith for her sons, the food of the soul, the pure and everlasting source of spiritual life.

PRAY

Dear Lord, thank you for speaking to me through the Bible. Please help me to acquire a taste for it, as I continue to feast upon the riches of your Word. Amen.

Days 12–18

SECOND WEEK
OF LENT

THOUGHT FOR THE WEEK

Do not be afraid. Open wide the doors for
Christ!

—St. John Paul II[4]

Day 12

DON'T GIVE UP!

Second Sunday of Lent

READ

> But Jesus came and touched them, saying,
> "Rise, and have no fear."
>
> —Matthew 17:7

REFLECT

Before the Transfiguration, Jesus told his followers of the need for self-denial and cross-carrying. Then he led Peter, James, and John to the top of a mountain and gave them a glimpse of the kingdom of God. They saw Jesus (in his heavenly glory) conversing with Moses and Elijah, and they heard the voice of God the Father.

Ultimately, this experience of the divine caused them to be afraid. In fact, St. Matthew wrote that hearing God's voice caused them to fall on their faces in awe (see Matthew 17:6). At this point, Jesus instructed them to rise and have no fear. It was time to descend from the mountain and get back to work.

Even though you've only been on this Lenten journey for a few weeks, there is a good chance you have fallen—either by giving way to worry or possibly by falling into serious sin. If that's the case, you are in the same place as Peter, James, and John—lying down and staring at the ground. If you continue to look downward, all you see is your failure. Doing this for any length of time could cause you to plunge into despair.

You may feel that you'll never succeed at moving away from worry and moving closer to Jesus. Nothing could be further from the truth. If this is your situation, you are actually in a very good place. You are in the same position as Peter, James, and John when Jesus approached and touched them. He speaks the same words to you that he spoke to them: "Rise, and have no fear." You can respond in one of two ways. Either you can continue to look downward and beat yourself up for having fallen or you can do what the three apostles did: "And when they lifted up their eyes, they saw no one but Jesus only" (Mt 17:8).

Whatever it is you are doing for Lent this year—whether you are trying to stop worrying, give up sweets, or lead a holy life—it is impossible to do it on your own. Eventually you will fail. But don't give up! Jesus will often let you stumble because he wants you to remember that you need him. It may feel like a bad thing when it happens, but it isn't. It's a reality check. You *do* need Jesus, and he wants you to turn to him.

RESPOND

Failing at Lenten resolutions does not mean that you're a bad person; it means that you're human. Those of us who tend to worry like to be in control. Today, let's focus on the fact that Jesus is the one in control of our lives. Every time we mess up, it gives us the opportunity to turn to him and ask for help. Let's do that today.

PRAY

Dear Jesus, thank you for always being there to pick me up whenever I fall. I can't do anything without your help. Please grant me the grace to move away from worrying and move closer to you. Amen.

DELIVERANCE

Monday—Second Week of Lent

READ

> I sought the LORD, and he answered me,
>   and delivered me from all my fears.
>   —Psalm 34:4

REFLECT

While I can't guarantee that you will be delivered from all of your fears by the time Easter Sunday rolls around, I can guarantee that seeking the Lord will bring you greater peace. When and how you put an end to worrying, once and for all . . . that is up to him.

That's the beauty of an intimate relationship. Once you invite Jesus Christ into your life, you begin an adventure that is entirely out of your hands. He is going to bless you in ways you can't imagine. One of those blessings will be an increased sense of peace. Just make sure that you don't get ahead of him. As this verse clearly states, he will answer your requests to be delivered from your fears. It will probably not happen overnight, however. If you can learn to accept that, you are well on your way to the peace you desire.

Here's something you may not have considered. The Lord has been pursuing you for much longer that you've been pursuing him. Why? Because he loves you. In the parable of the Lost Sheep (see Matthew 18:12–14, Luke 15:3–7), Jesus tells the story of the shepherd who leaves his ninety-nine sheep to seek out the one that was lost. It doesn't matter how many other people have surrendered their lives to him; Christ wants you and will do anything to get you. You are mistaken if you feel that the events in your life are happening by accident. All of the trials and suffering that you face every day are designed to draw you closer to him. If you are struggling with anxiety, rest assured that he is using it to call you.

The fact that you are reading this book indicates that you are responding to the Lord's call. There are plenty of self-help books that offer suggestions for conquering worry. You may even have read some of them. It should be obvious that this book is primarily about meeting Jesus. The Lord can help you stop worrying. Furthermore, you probably realize (or you will soon) that finding peace is not strictly an intellectual pursuit or a "mind over matter" process. It involves a daily encounter with Jesus Christ. That encounter is ultimately what will lead you to the peace you desire.

RESPOND

Remember the fears you brought to the Lord on day 4? Continue to ask him to deliver you from these fears and expect him to answer. Read and reread today's Bible verse until you begin to believe it in your heart. God always keeps his word. If you're skeptical, go ahead and tell him, but then ask for deliverance anyway. That's exactly what he wants.

PRAY

Lord, sometimes it's easier to worry about my fears than to ask you for help. I hate to admit it, but I often struggle to believe that you can help me. In spite of my doubts, I will ask anyway. I am afraid of the following things: (*list your fears*). Please handle them in the best way possible and help me to not be afraid. Amen.

Day 14

FRUITFUL WAITING

Tuesday—Second Week of Lent

READ

> Rejoice in your hope, be patient in tribulation, be constant in prayer.
>
> —Romans 12:12

REFLECT

I have a confession: Joy, patience, and consistency do not come easy for me. It's just not the way I'm wired. But that doesn't mean that I can't put St. Paul's instructions into practice. I can and I must—especially if I want to be peaceful.

Why do I rejoice? The answer is very simple. I rejoice because God loves me and desires to have an intimate relationship with me. Furthermore, he wants me to live with him forever in heaven.

How often do I forget this? Too many times to count. The exact number varies from day to day, but it is always equal to the number of times I complain or become discouraged about events in my life. The more we comprehend God's goodness, the easier it is to be joyful.

What about patience, especially in tribulation? I don't like to wait—period! It becomes even more difficult when I am suffering. Because of this character trait, it has been difficult for me to wait on the Lord. Once I decide that I want something, I typically want it yesterday. Unfortunately, that type of attitude will only lead to frustration. Learning to be patient with God, however, will bring peace.

So what's the secret to becoming more joyful and patient? The key that unlocks this entire verse is found at the end of the sentence: don't stop praying! If you want become more joyful and patient, it's extremely difficult to do on your own. Why not ask God for help? While any kind of prayer will bring you closer to the Lord, praying to overcome a specific weakness is a great idea.

If you're wondering to whom you should direct your prayer, try the Holy Spirit. St. Paul also reminds us, "The fruit of the Spirit is love, *joy*, *peace*, *patience*, kindness, goodness, faithfulness, gentleness, self-control" (Gal 5:22–23, emphasis mine).

Read the list again, and this time pay specific attention to the bolded words. Not only does the Holy Spirit specialize in joy and patience, he can give you peace as well. We'll talk more about his role tomorrow, but start asking him to help you today.

RESPOND

If you look at St. Paul's instruction as something you have to do on your own, it can seem overwhelming. The good news is neither Paul nor God expect you to do it on your own. I'll take it a step further and say that they absolutely, positively don't want you to do it by yourself. Today, ask the Holy Spirit

to help. If the prayer seems too simple, guess again. It's one of
the most powerful prayers you will ever pray!

PRAY

Come, Holy Spirit!

Day 15

ASK YOUR FATHER

Wednesday—Second Week of Lent

READ

> If you then, who are evil, know how to give good gifts to your children, how much more will the heavenly Father give the Holy Spirit to those who ask him!
>
> —Luke 11:13

REFLECT

Yesterday, we discussed the Holy Spirit and how he can assist us in many ways. Looking at the words of Jesus in today's Bible verse, we find that a few points emerge. First, it appears that we need to do something if we expect the Holy Spirit to work in our lives. Second, Jesus indicates that our heavenly Father will not deny our requests for the Holy Spirit, provided that we ask.

It sounds simple; doesn't it? In fact, it almost sounds too simple. We just can't wrap our brains around the fact that all we have to do is ask and we will receive. We think that it must be more complicated and forget to ask the Father for this great gift.

At this point, you may be questioning why you need to ask the Father for the Holy Spirit. Isn't the Spirit received in Baptism and strengthened in Confirmation? Yes, but just like Jesus, the Holy Spirit will not force his way into your life. Unless you invite him to become active, he will generally stand by, waiting patiently.

You may also wonder just how active he needs to be in your life. To answer that, I recommend you look at the previously mentioned list of the fruits of the Spirit: *love, joy, peace, patience, kindness, goodness, faithfulness, gentleness, and self-control.* (It's pretty eye-opening; isn't it?) Wouldn't you like to have more of these virtues in your life? I sure would!

Most of us will take one look at that list and realize that we need to take Jesus up on the offer and start asking the Father for an increase in the gifts of the Holy Spirit. And since we already know what his answer will be, we can take another look at that list of fruits and begin to see what we'll look like in the future. It's a very nice picture!

RESPOND

One of the themes you will see repeatedly in the pages of this book is "Do your best and let God do the rest." Learning to differentiate between God's role and your role makes life much easier. It will also give you the peace that you seek. He has his job and you have yours. We use the same prayer as yesterday, and it is by design. Sometimes we prefer our prayers to be long and drawn out, thinking that it will make them more effective. Not true. Inviting the Holy Spirit to act in your life can be done with just a few words. Get used to praying this prayer often. He will gradually transform your life so that the traits on that list don't seem so foreign to you.

PRAY

Come, Holy Spirit!

Day 16

FEAR VS. WORRY

Thursday—Second Week of Lent

READ

> But when he saw the wind, he was afraid,
> and beginning to sink he cried out, "Lord,
> save me."
>
> —Matthew 14:30

REFLECT

Sometimes we believe that being afraid is the same thing as worrying. That is completely untrue. *Fear is an emotion and worry is an action.* One we can control and the other we can't. The goal of this book is to help you stop worrying, not to keep you from being afraid. Before we dig into this Bible verse, let's take a closer look at fear and worry.

Fear is an emotion (sometimes referred to as a feeling or passion) that occurs when you feel threatened in some way. And, while this threat can be real or imaginary, the important thing to remember is that you can't control the feeling. According to the *Catechism*: "In themselves passions are neither good nor evil" (1767).

That takes some of the pressure off; doesn't it? Fear, in and of itself, is morally neutral. In other words, don't be afraid to be afraid! In the Bible, many holy people experienced fear, including Abraham (see Genesis 15:1), Moses (see Numbers 21:34), Mary (see Luke 1:30), Joseph (see Matthew 1:20), and Paul (see Acts 18:9). It is not a sin to be afraid.

What about worry? The dictionary typically defines it as giving way to anxiety or unease or allowing one's mind to dwell on difficulty or troubles. Although it may not feel like it at times, worrying is a voluntary action. You can choose to not worry. This is an extremely important concept to understand. You can't control the way you feel, but you can control how you respond to your feelings.

St. Peter was a fisherman and knew that it was not possible to walk on water. He was also a disciple of Jesus Christ and a witness to many miracles. Therefore, when the Lord invited him to get out of the boat and walk on water (see Matthew 14:22–33), Peter obeyed. As long as he stayed focused on Jesus, he remained above sea level. When he began to concentrate on the waves crashing around him, however, Peter became afraid and began to sink.

Now, if the story ended there, this would be a terrible example of how to respond to fear. But Peter reacted to the fear by crying out, "Lord, save me!" That is a prayer. In his fear, Peter turned to Jesus instead of worrying. That is exactly what we should do.

Will you?

RESPOND

Are we sometimes afraid when we shouldn't be? Absolutely. Let's put that aside for now and focus on how we should respond to the fear in our lives. Once again, I'll ask you to think of your fears. It may be uncomfortable, but it is necessary. Then picture Jesus standing in front of you and use the prayer composed by St. Peter when he was sinking.

PRAY

Lord, save me!

Day 17

"THANK YOU, LORD!"

Friday—Second Week of Lent

READ

> Fear not, O land;
>> be glad and rejoice,
>> for the LORD has done great things!
>>> —Joel 2:21

REFLECT

In previous meditations, I asked you to think about your greatest fears. Today I'd like you to look at something that is more pleasant but easily overlooked. Concentrate on all the great things the Lord has done, throughout history and in your own life. Unless you do this, you'll never have the confidence in God that is needed to stop worrying.

When it comes to the Lord and his greatness, there is hardly a shortage of descriptive examples to ponder. Here are just a few found in scripture:

- "In the beginning God created the heavens and the earth" (Gn 1:1).
- "Then Moses stretched out his hand over the sea; and the LORD drove the sea back by a strong east wind all night,

and made the sea dry land, and the waters were divided"
(Ex 14:21).

- "That evening they brought to him many who were pos-
  sessed with demons; and he cast out the spirits with a
  word, and healed all who were sick" (Mt 8:16).
- "And he awoke and rebuked the wind, and said to the
  sea, 'Peace! Be still!' And the wind ceased, and there was
  a great calm" (Mk 4:39).
- "When he had said this, he cried out with a loud voice,
  'Lazarus, come out.' The dead man came out, his hands
  and feet bound with bandages, and his face wrapped with
  a cloth" (Jn 11:43–44).
- "He is not here; for he has risen, as he said" (Mt 28:6).

These are just a few examples of great things done by the
Lord throughout history. The word powerful doesn't do him
justice. He can do anything. Who doesn't know that, right?

The problem is that we know it in our heads, but not in
our hearts. We discussed it on day 6, and yet we still need to
revisit it. When we get blindsided by a job loss, health scare,
or broken marriage, this knowledge sometimes goes out the
window and we plunge into despair. If you forget about God's
power, you will fail to turn to him in times of trouble. Once
that happens, you can forget about experiencing peace.

The Lord can handle your problems. Nothing is too big
for him. Furthermore, you are his child and he loves you with
an unconditional love. If you spend some time reflecting on
his track record, you'll understand how the prophet Joel could
say "Fear not, O land; be glad and rejoice"!

RESPOND

Find a quiet place and spend ten or fifteen minutes listing all of the great things the Lord has done in your life. You can start with creating you to live with him forever in heaven. Ask the Holy Spirit to guide your thoughts. You may be surprised at how long your list actually is.

PRAY

Thank you for your greatness, Lord. Help me to better appreciate your power so that I can turn to you with confidence instead of doubt. Amen.

Day 18

"TAKE MY HAND, LORD."

Saturday—Second Week of Lent

READ

> For I, the LORD your God,
>   hold your right hand;
> it is I who say to you, "Fear not,
>   I will help you."
>
> —Isaiah 41:13

REFLECT

When I host my daily morning show on Holy Spirit Radio in Philadelphia, I always sign off by saying, "Wherever you go today and whatever you do, the Lord is with you. Turn around and say, 'Hi.'" This phrase wasn't something that I thought about in advance. It just came out of my mouth one day, it seemed to fit, and I kept using it.

Those of us who are worry-prone very often forget about God's constant presence in our lives. This is a dangerous practice, and one that we need to correct. There are many ways to lose sight of the nearness of the Lord: when we fail to pray (or start daydreaming while praying), when we become preoccupied with everyday distractions, or when we give in to temptation (such as viewing inappropriate material on the internet). The list goes on and on—and all these things can cause us to turn our attention away from the One who loves us. And if we need to be reminded of that basic fact of his presence, there is no way that we're going to feel the comfort and support of his hand upon us, as Isaiah spoke of in the passage.

Think of it. Not only is the Lord with you as you read this, but also he is holding you by the hand and assuring you of his assistance. What kind of help does he offer? Whatever you need! If you're struggling with forgiveness, worry, lust, apathy, anger, job performance, marital issues, loneliness, or anything else, God wants to help. No wonder he told Isaiah to "fear not"! He wants to "roll up his sleeves" and get involved in your life. How involved? Consider this: "And the Word became flesh and dwelt among us" (Jn 1:14).

Jesus Christ—his Incarnation, his earthly ministry, and his Passion, Death, and Resurrection—is the Father's most eloquent expression of how close he wants to be to us. He is with you each day, holding your hand and offering to assist you. Will you let him?

RESPOND

Once again a common theme surfaces—Jesus wants to help you if you let him. Will you allow him to ease whatever burdens you are carrying today? If you're not inviting him to do this on a daily basis, please start today. Whether you feel him there or not, Jesus is by your side and holding your hand. He is waiting to help you with anything and everything. By the way, I'll give you some inside information—he's really good with impossible problems!

PRAY

Lord Jesus, thank you for walking beside me and holding my hand. Today, I surrender my life to you. Please help me to deal with everything that comes my way. Amen.

Days 19–25

THIRD WEEK
OF LENT

THOUGHT FOR THE WEEK

If you're experiencing stress or tension give it to Jesus. Tell Him, "I feel like crawling the wall, but I love You and I want to give this to You." Do you think our Lord wasn't tense living with those twelve screwball apostles?

—Mother Angelica[5]

Day 19

HIS TRANSFORMING PRESENCE

Third Sunday of Lent

READ

> One of his disciples, Andrew, Simon Peter's
> brother, said to him, "There is a lad here who
> has five barley loaves and two fish; but what
> are they among so many?"
>
> —John 6:8–9

REFLECT

Do you ever find yourself facing a challenging situation and
saying, "I can't do it" or "I'm not strong enough"? When we
are asked to do something difficult, it can be tempting to give
up before we even give it a try. This was true of those in the
Lord's inner circle as well—they were subject to this same
temptation!

When the disciples were faced with the dilemma of how
to feed five thousand hungry people, Jesus tested Philip by
posing the question, "How are we to buy bread, so that these
people may eat?" (Jn 6:5). The apostle responded by stating
that they didn't have enough money to buy the needed food.
Andrew acknowledged that they had some food (five loaves
and two fish) but concluded that it was not enough to feed
such a crowd.

Had they forgotten what had happened at the wedding in Cana, when Jesus turned water into wine? For some reason, it never even occurred to them to ask for the Lord's assistance. Then, as if to remind them, Jesus multiplied the loaves and fish so that all could eat. Now, before we get too focused on the happy ending and write this off as "just another miracle," let's concentrate on a few key points.

Did you notice how Jesus didn't just create the food out of thin air? He could have, but he chose not to. Instead, he accepted the young boy's offering of five loaves and two fish— which wasn't enough—and multiplied them so that it was more than enough. *When we are faced with a challenge, Jesus expects us to do our best and let him do the rest.*

The second point is that the Lord's actions in this account foreshadow the miracle of the Eucharist: At every Mass the Lord miraculously transforms the bread and wine into his real presence, offering himself to us, Body and Blood, soul and divinity. He takes ordinary ingredients (the best we can offer) and transforms them in order to come to us in the most intimate way possible. When you receive Holy Communion, you get the grace that will allow you to deal with any problem imaginable.

RESPOND

As we celebrate the Lord's day today, you've had or will have the opportunity to receive Jesus in the Eucharist. Spend some time in silent gratitude, thanking him for the gift of his presence. By yourself, you can't deal with the significant challenges of life or find peace in a crazy world. Fortunately, you aren't being asked to do it by yourself. Jesus is available in the Eucharist and wants to help you. What an incredible gift!

PRAY

Dear Jesus, I am not strong enough to deal with the problems that face me each day, but I know you can help me. Please allow me to receive all the graces contained in the Eucharist and deliver me from all my fears. Amen.

Day 20

STRENGTH IN WEAKNESS

Monday—Third Week of Lent

READ

> I can do all things in him who strengthens
> me.
>
> —Philippians 4:13

REFLECT

This is one of the most powerful, yet misunderstood verses in the Bible. It doesn't mean we can do anything. No matter how hard I try, there are some things that I will never be able to do. I will never be able to sing professionally, play in the NFL, or become a *Jeopardy!* champion. It's just not realistic to imagine that I will ever be able to do any of these things.

There is some good news here, however: with God's help, you will be able to do anything he calls you to do. When you're looking at an unexpected tragedy or apparently hopeless dilemma, that's exactly the kind of news you need to hear. (This is a great example of the relevance and practicality of the Bible.) St. Paul wrote these words while he was sitting in a Roman prison. He had just finished explaining how he learned to be content in any situation because he discovered the source of all happiness—Jesus Christ. His relationship with the Lord was all that mattered. Because of the presence of

Christ in his life, Paul didn't worry about what was happening to him. Instead, he believed that he could handle anything that came his way. The better you know Jesus, the less you will worry. How do we get to that point? As I emphasize throughout this book, prayer and scripture are essential. You cannot get to know the Lord without using these tools. But these two practices are not enough. Jesus knew that, and that is why he gave us the sacraments. According to Pope Francis, we must celebrate "Jesus in the Sacraments, for it is there that he gives us life, nourishes us, comforts us, makes a covenant with us, gives us a mission. Without the celebration of the Sacraments, we will not arrive at the knowledge of Jesus." [6]

Want to know Jesus better? It can only be accomplished through prayer, scripture, and the sacraments. Focusing exclusively on the first two makes the process more about us and less about Jesus. In order to truly know him, we need his help. The grace received in the sacraments is critical.

RESPOND

You are not going to develop the faith of St. Paul overnight. Take it one day at a time. How often do you receive the Eucharist and go to Confession? If possible, try to increase the frequency this Lent. Also, start asking for an increase in the graces given in the other sacraments you have received. It will make a big difference in your life.

PRAY

Dear Jesus, thank you for your presence in the sacraments. Please pour out the grace that I need to face any situation I encounter. Amen.

Day 21

DON'T LOSE HOPE!

Tuesday—Third Week of Lent

READ

> And he looked up and said, "I see men; but they look like trees, walking." Then again he laid his hands upon his eyes; and he looked intently and was restored, and saw everything clearly.
>
> —Mark 8:24–25

REFLECT

After laying his hands on a blind man in Bethsaida, Jesus asked, "Do you see anything?" (Mk 8:23). The man's response, recorded in the verse at the top of the page, is rather perplexing. What went wrong? Why didn't the healing "take" the first time? Could it be that Jesus didn't say the right words or touch the man for the correct amount of time?

Not at all. What we find here is something that should give you great hope. This encounter reminds us that Jesus often heals us in stages. More often than not, healing is a process that takes time. Remembering this will spare you much grief and prevent you from giving up when your prayers aren't answered quickly enough.

Even if you finish this book and follow the directions to the letter, you may still lapse into worrying after Lent is over. I can say with a great deal of confidence that you will probably worry less than before, but you may still slip up from time to time. That is okay. It doesn't necessarily mean you messed up or that the Lord is not listening to your prayers. Healing is not something we do on our own. It depends on God, and his timing is always perfect. If he makes you wait, there is a reason. Like the blind man who was in the process of being healed, it's important that you learn to recognize little signs that indicate God is working in your life.

Do you think that you picked up this book because *you* want to stop worrying? I don't. I believe that the Holy Spirit urged you to do it. He wants you to stop worrying even more than you do. And what is it that has given you the persistence to keep reading this book for the past twenty days? Is it sheer willpower—or the grace of God to persevere? In the past few weeks, have you felt peace in the midst of turmoil? Even a little bit of peace? That's yet another sign that God is up to something. Don't give up. Those "walking trees" will be looking like men before you know it!

RESPOND

Spend ten minutes today in silent prayer, asking the Holy Spirit to give you some examples of how God is helping you in your battle to overcome worry. Be careful. The signs could be very small, so you may have to look closely. We are nearing the halfway point of Lent, so I'm reasonably sure you will see something.

PRAY

Jesus, thank you for responding to my cry of help this Lent. I'm grateful that you are working in my life. Please help me to persevere so that I may grow even closer to you. Amen.

Day 22

LIFE CAN BE TOUGH!

Wednesday—Third Week of Lent

READ

> I have said this to you, that in me you may
> have peace. In the world you have tribula-
> tion; but be of good cheer, I have overcome
> the world.
>
> —John 16:33

REFLECT

We can always trust Jesus to tell it like it is, whether we like it or not. In this case, he reminds us that we will encounter problems and suffering in this world. Everyone will experience suffering at some point, sometimes even horrific suffering. The Holocaust, the World Trade Center attack, and the Sandy Hook Elementary School massacre are just a few examples. And yet, when Jesus issued this ominous warning, in the very next breath he delivered a consoling message: "But be of good cheer, I have overcome the world."

The key to understanding this message can be found in the last five words. Bad things will happen in the world. People will suffer and die. And yet, there is a bigger picture that must be grasped if we are ever to find peace. Our life on earth is temporary. It will come to an end in a relatively short period of time. We were created to live with the Lord forever in paradise. When Jesus died on the Cross and rose from the dead, the gates of heaven were opened for us, once and for all.

None of us like to suffer. In fact, one of the main reasons we worry is our fear of suffering. Worrying is a kind of defense mechanism that helps us to prepare for anything unpleasant that could possibly happen. It's not a productive use of our time, however, and actually moves us away from the Lord.

Wouldn't it be better if we could be unaffected by the difficulties that come our way? Essentially, that is what Jesus is promising in this Bible verse. He is bigger than any potential problem that you can encounter. While he isn't saying that you will never shed a tear or feel queasy in your stomach, he is saying that you can find peace in him. Don't panic if you're not there yet. By the time you finish this book, you'll be closer to that peace than you are now. Just keep focused on the Prince of Peace and you will get there.

RESPOND

It's time to make a decision. Do you want to believe the words of Jesus Christ, or do you want to believe the message of the world? Spend some time reflecting on the Lord's words in John 16:33. Do you believe them? If not, it's okay. Pray the simple prayer that follows and expect him to answer. Express the desire to believe what he is saying. Doing so will be infinitely more productive than worrying about what might happen in the future.

PRAY

Lord Jesus, I'm tired of worrying about what might happen in the future. Help me to believe that you are bigger than any problem I will ever face. Amen.

Day 23

PUTTING LIMITS ON GOD

Thursday—Third Week of Lent

READ

> Behold, I am the LORD, the God of all flesh;
> is anything too hard for me?
>
> —Jeremiah 32:27

REFLECT

Is anything too hard for God? Now honestly, how would you answer this question? We all know that nothing is too difficult for God, but our thoughts and actions rarely reflect that belief. By its very nature, worrying expresses doubt in God's power and goodness. For some reason, our belief in an all-powerful God doesn't carry over to the concerns of daily life. We accept the fact that he created the entire universe out of nothing, but struggle to believe that he can find us a job or cure our chronic pain. What gives?

Much of the difficulty arises when we view the Lord in an impersonal manner. Rather than seeing him as someone who wants to be involved in our lives, we view him as some sort of CEO who is in the creation and miracle business. In other words, he's too big to be concerned with our little problems. Not only is this untrue, it's also damaging to our relationship. In order for you to approach him confidently in prayer, you need to believe that God is just as concerned with your need to find a parking spot as he is with bringing peace to the world. Obviously, the problems are not of equal importance, but his concern is. He cares about you as if you were the only person alive.

How can you learn to truly believe this? It takes time, but it can be done. I recommend that you start by focusing on the fact God loves you so much that he sent his only Son into the world so that you could have eternal life (see John 3:16). Even though it involved tremendous suffering, Jesus died on the Cross that you could go to heaven. He gave up his life for you. And in his own words, "Greater love has no man than this, that a man lay down his life for his friends" (Jn 15:13).

He cares about you, and nothing is too difficult for him. Are you ready to give him a chance?

RESPOND

Once again, I encourage you to answer the Lord's question with a simple yes or no. Is anything too hard for him? Now, let's take it a step further. Think of the single most impossible problem in your life. You may have many problems, but let's start with one for now. Present it to the Lord and ask him to fix it. Do it even if you don't feel that it is fixable. Ignore any feelings of uncertainty or skepticism and ask him to handle it. Sometimes we are afraid to ask because we don't want to be disappointed. Your faith will never grow if you use that approach. Give the Lord the chance to perform a miracle in your life. Do it today!

PRAY

Dear Jesus, it's often easier to worry about my problems than to ask you for help. Today, I will give you a chance to show your power in my life by asking you to fix (*mention your problem*). Thank you!

Day 24

JESUS LOVES YOU . . . ALWAYS!

Friday—Third Week of Lent

READ

> Who shall separate us from the love of Christ? Shall tribulation, or distress, or persecution, or famine, or nakedness, or peril, or sword?
>
> —Romans 8:35

REFLECT

Yesterday, we focused on the great love that Jesus has for each of us. The thought of his unconditional love can be very comforting. As human beings, we tend to be a lot less constant in our affections. We are filled with gratitude on the days he answers our prayers by granting us what we ask. On the other hand, it's easy to get a bit rattled when a request is denied. Does that mean he no longer loves us?

Let's begin by asking the question: What is love? Is it merely a warm feeling, or the simple act of doing something nice for someone? Actually, it's a lot more than that. While it is true that those things can accompany love, this definition ignores the most important aspect. Quoting St. Thomas Aquinas, the *Catechism of the Catholic Church* states that "to love is to will the good of another" (1766).

Failing to understand that God wills our good, and only our good, can cause major problems in the spiritual life. Doubting God's love robs us of the peace that God wants for us. And so, we must remind ourselves continually: *True love means willing good for the beloved.*

Yes, Christ loves you unconditionally. I have more good news for you as well: he always wants what is best for you, and his divinity allows him to correct any problems that arise in your life. Because he can do all things, nothing is off the table for him. Curing cancer, stopping a tornado, restoring sight to the blind—all of these things are possible for him.

Now, I know what you're thinking. It's the obvious elephant in the room: If God can do all these things, then why is there so much suffering in the world? If the Lord can always do something about our suffering, why doesn't he?

Take a moment and read today's scripture passage again. St. Paul's words are very clear—nothing can separate us from the love of Christ. If you are going through tough times, the Lord is allowing it; your trials are an expression of his love for you. If you get nothing else out of this book, please remember this fact. You don't have to feel it and you don't have to like it, but you need to believe it: Jesus loves you and everything that is happening (or will happen) in your life is a manifestation of that love. We'll dig into the meaning of suffering in the fifth week of Lent.

RESPOND

Today's message may frustrate you or make you angry. That's not a bad thing, depending on how you handle it. I invite you to spend ten or fifteen minutes speaking to the Lord about the suffering in your life. Use Paul's message to the Romans as a starting point. If you're frustrated, tell it to Jesus. He wants to hear from you and he loves honesty. As my spiritual director used to say, "Go ahead and tell Jesus how you really feel. He can take it."

PRAY

Dear Lord, it's difficult to understand how my trials are an expression of your love. It just doesn't make sense to me. Please help me to understand. Amen.

Day 25

"MARTHA, MARTHA . . ."

Saturday—Third Week of Lent

READ

> But the Lord answered her, "Martha, Martha, you are anxious and troubled about many things; one thing is needful. Mary has chosen the good portion, which shall not be taken away from her."
>
> —Luke 10:41–42

REFLECT

It's hard to read the story of Martha and Mary (see Luke 10:38–42) without feeling some sympathy for Martha. When Jesus came to the home of the two sisters, he was received in two vastly different ways. Mary sat at the Lord's feet and listened to his teaching while Martha was distracted with getting dinner ready. At first glance it appears that Martha was being a good hostess while Mary was a bit of a slacker. Yet when she complained to Jesus about Mary's inactivity, Martha received that surprising response from Jesus.

What gives? Isn't the Lord being a little unfair?

The key to understanding this story can be found by looking carefully at the scripture passage. St. Luke describes Martha as being "distracted with much serving," and Jesus refers to her as "anxious and troubled." It wasn't so much Martha's hospitality that drew the Lord's reprimand, but her state of mind. Martha focused more on the act of serving than the person whom she was serving.

What could she have done differently? She could have been a little more Mary-like. While Martha was running around frantically, Mary sat at the feet of Jesus and enjoyed his company. She recognized the great gift of his presence.

Now, I have a type A personality. It's not easy for me to sit still when things need to get done. Martha had the same tendency. She was so eager to take care of business that she was not about to stop for anything—even to spend time with Jesus. This poor decision caused her to become anxious and troubled. I have seen the same result in my life and guarantee you will too. Failing to spend time with the Lord each day is a surefire way to make your life more stressful.

Spending time in prayer seems insane when we have a million things to do, but that's generally because we underestimate its power. Jesus said that apart from him we can do nothing (see John 15:5), and he wasn't kidding. Yes, it's important to be prudent when deciding how much time to spend in prayer, but it should never be neglected. Time spent with the Lord in prayer is never wasted. It will make you not only more peaceful but more productive too.

RESPOND

Make the commitment to spend a fixed amount of time each day in conversation with Jesus. How much time? Ten minutes is a great place to start. You can always pray more if you want, but make it a point to never skip your daily prayer time. You can change the hour, the location, or the method, but don't pass up the opportunity to spend time with the Lord.

PRAY

Dear Jesus, I promise to spend some time with you in prayer each day. Help me to remain faithful to that promise. Amen.

Days 26-32

FOURTH WEEK OF LENT

THOUGHT FOR THE WEEK

Abandon yourself totally in the arms of the divine goodness of the Heavenly Father and do not fear, because your fear would be more ridiculous than that of a child in his mother's womb.

—St. Padre Pio[7]

Day 26

WE'RE ALMOST THERE

Fourth Sunday of Lent

READ

> Rejoice with Jerusalem, and be glad for her,
>> all you who love her;
> rejoice with her in joy,
>> all you who mourn over her.
>
> —Isaiah 66:10

REFLECT

Today is Laetare Sunday, a day when our focus shifts to the "light at the end of the tunnel"—the Resurrection of Jesus! (*Laetare* means "rejoice" in Latin.) With that in mind, it's an appropriate time for us to imagine a life with less worry and greater trust in God. As I mentioned earlier in the book, we'll leave the "how" up to the Lord. Our job today is to picture how good it will be to live a life filled with peace.

As I write this, we are coming to the end of a cold and snowy winter. There is still a chill in the morning air, but the weather forecast is calling for temperatures in the 70s by the end of the week. I am looking forward to that. On my way out the front door today, I consoled myself with the thought of the warmth that will be heading our way. We should learn to take the same approach when it comes to the misery caused by anxiety. No matter how much you worry, there is hope. Jesus can and will help you if you continue to turn to him.

Today's Bible verse offers the promise of hope for the future. Things might not be looking good at the moment, but they will get better. That is the message the Lord has for you on this Laetare Sunday. You may still be overwhelmed by your problems and trapped in the prison of anxiety, but it will get better. I can't promise you when and I can't promise how much better, but I believe in the healing power of Jesus Christ. If you continue to walk with him each day throughout Lent, you can expect something to change by the time Easter rolls around. That is reason enough to rejoice!

RESPOND

I have a feeling that you're going to enjoy today's activity. Since today is a day focused on looking ahead to Easter Sunday, spend some time thanking the Lord for what he is about to do in your life. You know that he doesn't want you to worry. You are also aware that he wants to help you. Therefore, you can be sure that your prayers will not go unanswered. Turn to him in Thanksgiving and get ready to experience a change.

PRAY

Thank you, Lord, for helping me to break free from anxiety. I understand that it will be a lifelong process and that I need to take one day at a time, but I expect to see some improvement by the end of Lent. Only you know how significant the change will be, and I will trust that you will give me just what I need. I am grateful. Amen.

Day 27

SPIRITUAL JUNK FOOD

Monday—Fourth Week of Lent

READ

> Do not labor for the food which perishes,
> but for the food which endures to eternal
> life, which the Son of man will give to you;
> for on him has God the Father set his seal.
> —John 6:27

REFLECT

Do you tend to fall back on certain coping strategies when you're feeling anxious—habits that are not particularly good for you, spiritually speaking? I am a veteran of pursuing this kind of perishable "food," especially when it comes to my quest for peace. Over the course of my life, I have spent countless hours watching TV, pursuing wealth, listening to music, eating junk food, collecting sports memorabilia, and consuming alcoholic beverages in an attempt to escape from anxiety. And I know that I am not alone. Millions of people are doing the same thing every day. One of the greatest myths ever invented is that happiness can be found in material goods. That is a flat-out lie. Things may make you forget about your problems for a while, but not for long.

The pursuit of material goods as a source of happiness is not a new problem. There was a reason that Jesus first spoke these words two thousand years ago. The desire for instant gratification and freedom from suffering is a result of our fallen human nature. But while it may not be a new problem in the twenty-first century, it is a bigger temptation than it has been at any point in history. We live in an extremely distracting and noisy world. Technology has made it possible to be bombarded with the same message wherever we go: the more things you have, the happier you will be.

I can tell you firsthand that this message is a lie. I spent thousands of dollars trying to buy happiness, and it didn't work. If anything, I became even more depressed because it was difficult to keep up the pace. Finding new toys and sources of pleasure became more difficult, especially since I didn't have an unlimited source of funding.

Trying to find happiness by pursuing material goods is a mistake. It will not work. Lasting peace can only be found in Jesus Christ. Don't waste your time pursuing perishable goods. The Bible verse at the beginning of this day comes from what is known as the Bread of Life Discourse. In this address, Jesus reveals how he will make himself present in the Eucharist. Carrying the seal of his Father, Jesus Christ offers himself as a visible manifestation of an invisible God. This was a radical teaching that caused some to walk away from him. By doing so, they chose to embrace perishable food and forgo everlasting happiness. Today you are called to make a similar decision. What will you choose?

RESPOND

How do you deal with stress? Running away from your problems or drowning your sorrows will only get you so far. Make time today to open up your Bible and read the entire Bread of Life Discourse in John 6. Take your time and let the words of Jesus Christ speak to your heart. Unless you become intimate friends with him, you will never find peace.

PRAY

Lord Jesus, take away my desire to turn to material things when I'm feeling down. Help me to believe that you are the only lasting source of peace. Amen.

Day 28

LOOK FOR LITTLE SIGNS

Tuesday—Fourth Week of Lent

READ

> At the seventh time he said, "Behold, a little cloud like a man's hand is rising out of the sea." And he said, "Go up, say to Ahab, 'Prepare your chariot and go down, lest the rain stop you.'"
>
> —1 Kings 18:44

REFLECT

Despite the fact that the Bible documents many instances of Jesus performing miracles, we still struggle to believe that he can help us in an emergency. We might not want to admit it, but this disbelief is lived out whenever we worry. If we truly trusted in his power, there wouldn't be a reason to worry. Here's the great thing about the Lord. He knows that we don't trust him and wants to help us. He often does that through miracles.

Unfortunately, we sometimes fail to see the Lord working miraculously in our lives. This may happen because we're skeptical or it may occur because the miracles are rather ordinary. We sometimes attribute them to luck or happenstance, instead of divine intervention. The prophet Elijah knew better.

When he prayed for rain in the midst of a three-and-a-half-year drought, the smallest fist-shaped cloud was all he needed to see. He knew that the dry spell was over and acted accordingly. The rain was on its way! Are you walking through the desert right now with no end in sight? Sometimes all it takes is a little pondering and some help from the Holy Spirit. You may suddenly discover that the Lord really is at work in your life.

RESPOND

What are you praying for right now? Does it seem like God is ignoring your requests? Take some time and look for a sign that he is responding to your prayers. Ask the Holy Spirit to help you. You might have to look very closely, but I'm confident you'll find something. It might be as simple as recognizing that the problem hasn't gotten any worse or that you mysteriously feel more hopeful. We often miss the subtle ways that the Lord is operating in our lives. More often than not, he works in ordinary and not extraordinary ways. When you find the tiniest sign that he is responding to your prayers, thank him and keep praying.

PRAY

Dear Lord, open my eyes so I can see how you are working in my life. Amen.

Day 29

DO YOU TRUST GOD?

Wednesday—Fourth Week of Lent

READ

> You keep him in perfect peace,
>> whose mind is stayed on you,
>> because he trusts in you.
>
> —Isaiah 26:3, RSV:2CE

REFLECT

In order to be at peace, we must learn to trust God. If it sounds simple, that's because it is. And yet, the fact that trusting God is simple doesn't necessarily mean it is easy. Speaking as a lifelong worrier, I can assure you that trusting God can be a very difficult task. The good news is that it is possible, though you will have to work at it. Not only *can* you learn to trust him but also you *must* learn to trust him. Otherwise, you will never experience lasting peace in your life.

Now I have to tell you something that may sound discouraging: you can't force yourself to trust God. I know, it sounds crazy, right? How can you learn to trust God without forcing yourself to do it? This kind of trust develops over time, in small increments. Rather than forcing yourself to do something you can't do (trusting God), concentrate on doing something that you can do (controlling your thoughts and turning to him in prayer). Doing this faithfully with the smaller challenges of your life will gradually enable you to trust him for the big things.

We discussed thought control on day 2, but it is definitely worth revisiting. In order to stop worrying, you must learn to control your thoughts. Instead of imagining all the things that could go wrong, use your imagination to reinforce the truth: God is present and ready to help you.

As an example, picture Jesus standing before you. A big smile appears on his face when he sees you, and he motions you to come close to him. Imagine yourself being wrapped in his loving arms as he holds you tight. Think about him softly saying, "Relax. You are safe in my arms. Nothing can harm you. It's so good to be with you. Please stay with me for awhile." Now, say something to him in response. Ask him for whatever you need or tell him why you're afraid. Try to imagine how he would respond. Didn't that feel good? That exercise may only have lasted a few minutes, but it was definitely more pleasant than worrying.

Wait a minute, you might think. *Wasn't that just a religious version of "thinking happy thoughts"?* Not at all. It was an encounter with Jesus Christ. And the best news of all is that this encounter can take place whenever you desire. The Lord is always ready and willing to meet you. And guess what happens when you meet with him regularly? You guessed it. Your trust in him will increase. Why not give it a try and see what happens?

RESPOND

One of my favorite images of Jesus is the one given to St. Faustina Kowalska as part of the Divine Mercy revelation. At the bottom of the image are the words, "Jesus, I trust in you." Find a copy of that image (see TheDivineMercy.org) and slowly repeat those words. Keep doing it, and notice the peace that fills your heart. That simple exercise has brought me great peace, especially when I was on the verge of despair.

PRAY

Jesus, I trust in you.

Day 30

THE JOY OF KNOWING JESUS

Thursday—Fourth Week of Lent

READ

> And they worshiped him, and returned to
> Jerusalem with great joy, and were continu-
> ally in the temple blessing God.
> —Luke 24:52–53, RSV:2CE

REFLECT

With these words, the Gospel of Luke draws to a close. Jesus
had risen from the dead and was getting ready to return to
his Father. He instructed the apostles to go out into the world
and make disciples of all nations, sharing everything they had
been taught. He then ascended into heaven. The apostles were
left alone to deliver a message to a world that would want to
kill them. Now, go back and read the above Bible passage
again. Wow!

Forty days earlier, Jesus' disciples had been trying to save
their lives by hiding from the authorities. As the gospel closes,
they are rejoicing and seemingly unafraid to die. What caused
this radical transformation? It's hard to believe that this is the
same group of men. They went from being cowardly to coura-
geous in a very short amount of time. Obviously, something
happened to cause this change. Let's explore it more deeply.

If we begin to understand what took place in their lives, we can better put it to work in our own.

The gospels recount several incidents that changed these worriers into warriors. First, the Resurrection: they were obviously affected by the Lord's rising from the dead. Until he appeared to them in the Upper Room, they hid in fear—apparently forgetting the fact that he told them this was the plan. Not long after this, they received the gift of the Holy Spirit, along with the authority to forgive sins (see John 20:21–23). That was a *big* deal! Finally, St. Luke records that, just before ascending into heaven, Jesus lifted up his hands and blessed them (see Luke 24:50). When you add all of these events together, the apostles were equipped to handle their mission and *knew it*!

What does that mean for us? Listen up, because it's good news! Through the Sacraments of Baptism and Confirmation, we receive the Holy Spirit and all of his gifts. Those gifts are strengthened by the reception of the Eucharist and Reconciliation. When you read the Bible, the Lord speaks to you just as he did to the apostles, and when you attend Mass or pray before the Blessed Sacrament, you are in the real presence of Jesus—just like the apostles. You too can be joyful if you tap into those endless sources of grace.

RESPOND

Do you wish you had the apostles' ability to be joyful in the midst of hardship and persecution? Do something about it! Pray to the Holy Spirit, read a Bible passage, receive the sacraments, and ask the Lord to increase your joy. Ultimately, he will be the one to make it happen. Your job is to ask and take advantage of what he provides.

PRAY

Lord, please grant me the ability to be joyful at all times. You gave this gift to the apostles, and I know you will give it to me. Thank you.

Day 31

CAN IT REALLY BE THIS SIMPLE?

Friday—Fourth Week of Lent

READ

> Draw near to God and he will draw near to
> you.
>
> —James 4:8

REFLECT

Do you sometimes feel that getting to know God is a difficult process? He can't be seen or heard with our natural senses, the way we encounter other people. Sometimes we feel as though we are unworthy to speak to him, and that he operates in mysterious ways we could never possibly understand. We think it's necessary to use the right words and repeat them for the specified number of times in order to get his attention.

This simple verse blows all of those theories to smithereens!

It is not difficult to get close to God. One of the reasons the process is so simple is that he is with us wherever we go. The psalmist expresses it perfectly:

> Where shall I go from your Spirit?
>> Or where shall I flee from your presence?
> If I ascend to heaven, you are there!

> If I make my bed in Sheol, you are there! (Ps
> 139:7–8, RSV:2CE).

Even if we choose to ignore him, the Lord will still remain with us at all times. While that is a comforting thought, we shouldn't view it as a call to be complacent. God just doesn't want to accompany us through life—he wants to have an intimate relationship with us. And as with any relationship, it requires work from both parties. Don't worry about the Lord not holding up his end of the relationship. He's got it covered. We need to make sure that we do our part.

If you make the effort to grow close to the Lord, he will definitely respond. The best part is that he will not be outdone in generosity. Every minute spent in prayer will yield tremendous blessings. You may not be able to see the grace that you receive, but it is undoubtedly there. Time spent in prayer is never wasted. If you make the effort to draw close to the Lord, he will draw even closer to you.

RESPOND

Because this verse is so simple, there is a danger that it can be ignored. That would be a mistake. The Lord loves you so much that he gave you the gift of free will. Even though he wants to have an intimate relationship with you, he will not force you to do anything against your will. If you choose to ignore his offer of friendship, he will allow you to do so. That is how I lived my life for many years. The Lord was right there with me, and I pretended that he didn't exist. Since there's no time like the present, I'd like to ask you to pray the following prayer, put the book down, and then spend ten minutes focusing on the Lord's presence in your life. You can speak, listen or just sit quietly. He is with you right now. Enjoy some quality time with him.

PRAY

Thank you for your presence in my life, Lord. Please draw nearer to me. Amen.

Day 32

SOMEONE NEEDS YOUR HELP

Saturday—Fourth Week of Lent

READ

> Blessed be the God and Father of our Lord
> Jesus Christ, the Father of mercies and God
> of all comfort, who comforts us in all our
> affliction, so that we may be able to com-
> fort those who are in any affliction, with the
> comfort with which we ourselves are com-
> forted by God.
>
> —2 Corinthians 1:3–4

REFLECT

This is going to sound radical, but I must caution you about something before we go any further. Once you encounter God and experience his peace, you must be willing to share it with others. It's part of the deal.

Initially, I turned to Christ for the same reason you are reading this book: because I was looking for peace. You want to learn how the Lord can help you to stop worrying. But there's a catch: Once you turn to Jesus to alleviate your anxiety, it's important to remember that others are struggling and are searching for peace too. Jesus wants to help us, but he also expects us to help those around us.

All of my work (books, radio and TV programs, ministries at parishes) contains the same core message: Jesus. I want to share the Gospel of Jesus Christ with as many people as possible. Did I have this desire when I first turned to the Lord in an attempt to overcome my anxiety? No way! I was desperate and needed him to help me. Helping others wasn't on my mind. Don't panic if you feel the same way. It is extremely common. Most people surrender to the Lord because they need something. He understands that and will not hold it against you. In fact, he often uses ailments such as anxiety to get our attention.

Jesus knows that many of us would ignore him unless we feel like we can get something from him. It sounds nasty, but it's true. The only time this can be a problem is if we don't progress from the "What can you do for me?" mentality. An encounter with the love of Christ should ultimately inspire us to share the Good News with others.

There are other people in your life who need to hear about Jesus. If you don't think you're qualified to tell them about him, guess again! There are many worriers in the world who would never think to read a book on how the Lord can help them to experience peace. Some of those individuals are living under your roof. You are way ahead of the curve. Share Jesus with them . . . starting with this book!

RESPOND

The best way to start bringing comfort to those around you is by praying for them. If you feel it would help them to know that you are praying, then tell them. You can also simply let them know that you're available if they need to talk. Often your mere presence will be enough.

Identify three people who need to be comforted by the love of Jesus Christ (ask the Holy Spirit to help you), and commit to praying for them each day. Then look for an opening to help them in some way.

PRAY

Dear Jesus, thank you for comforting me. Please increase my desire to share you with others. Amen.

Days 33–39

FIFTH WEEK
OF LENT

THOUGHT FOR THE WEEK

Shake off excessive worry and exercise a little
confidence in God's providence!
—Bl. Solanus Casey[8]

Day 33

DON'T BE AFRAID TO SURRENDER

Fifth Sunday of Lent

READ

A man's mind plans his way,
   but the LORD directs his steps.
—Proverbs 16:9

REFLECT

As a worrier, I like to be in control. Therefore, it only makes sense that I'm a planner. We have previously discussed that worrying is a way to remain in control. Accounting for every potential negative outcome somehow alleviates the sense of fear about an unknown future. That's the theory, but we all know that the results are anything but comforting. Nevertheless, it does seem reasonable to conclude that worrying is an attempt to mitigate uncertainty. Lack of control is just not fun. At the risk of stating the obvious, however, none of us are ever truly in control. The sooner we learn to accept that, the more peaceful we will be.

There's an old Yiddish proverb, "Man plans and God laughs." Sound familiar? Even though it has happened to me countless times, I still continue to get frustrated when it occurs. You'd think I would have learned by now. Many of us struggle with relinquishing control of our plans to God. How can we overcome this hurdle? Proverbs 16:9 provides a good starting point.

God loves you and always desires what is best for you. Even though it may not seem like it at times, everything that happens in your life is designed to help you in some way. God is also all-powerful. He can do anything. In addition, he can prevent things from happening. You can rest assured that the events in your life have been approved by the Lord. He doesn't will evil, of course, but he does allow it to happen. Whether we realize it or not, he is constantly directing our steps. We can "hear" his voice through the daily circumstances of life. Although it can be very challenging, learning to listen to him in this manner can be very beneficial.

When your plans don't work out, God is telling you that he has a better plan. Just like a parent guiding a child away from a hot stove or a busy street, our heavenly Father often steers us away from potential trouble. His goal is to draw us close to him and lead us to heaven. Think about this when your plans don't work out. It's one of the many ways that God says, "I love you."

RESPOND

In order to get better at "hearing" God's voice in your disrupted plans, I recommend that you start by working on the little annoyances that you encounter today. When you're stuck in traffic, feeling a little off, or bummed out because it's raining, chalk it up to God's will. A concrete way to do this is by literally saying "Father, your will be done." You can also refrain from complaining. Finally, you can offer it up and unite your suffering with that of Christ. If you can learn to do this with the minor inconveniences that come your way, you will soon be able to do it when you encounter the big things.

PRAY

Lord, please help me to see your presence in everything that happens to me today, especially those things that are unpleasant. Amen.

Day 34

YOU ARE NEVER ALONE

Monday—Fifth Week of Lent

READ

> Be strong and of good courage; be not fright-
> ened, neither be dismayed; for the LORD
> your God is with you wherever you go.
>
> —Joshua 1:9

REFLECT

While growing up in Philadelphia, I spent a great deal of time playing stickball on the street. Even though my friends and I played on a side street that didn't have much traffic, we would have to contend with the occasional car that needed to get through. Because we were kids and believed that our game was the most important thing in the world, we didn't always step aside with lightning-fast speed.

While normally it wasn't a problem, one day a teenage driver (much bigger than any of us) got out of the car and told us that we should stay out of "his" street. After some tough talk and moderate pushing, our adversary got back in his car and drove off. One of my friends told his older (and more physically imposing) brother, who was upset about the altercation. He offered to stay with us the next time we played ball and promised he would take care of any problems that came up. True to his word, the older brother showed up, got out of his car, and stood there as we played our game of stickball. Even though I was a skinny weakling, I felt confident and hoped that our bully friend would come back. The mere presence of our guardian was enough to take away my fear. It wasn't what he said; it wasn't what he did; it was simply the fact that he was there.

For the Chosen People, Moses was like that older brother, guiding the Hebrews out of bondage and toward freedom. Just before they entered the Promised Land, the mantle of leadership passed from Moses to Joshua, who had the unenviable task of taking over for Moses. Talk about having big shoes to fill! After appointing Joshua to this important mission, the Lord assured the young leader that he would not be alone. That same promise is extended to each of us through this Bible verse. No matter what challenge we face in life, the Lord is standing next to us.

We are afraid because we can't see the big picture. God is always in control and will never desert us. You may encounter frightening situations and undergo suffering, but he is there. God will strengthen and uphold you in times of trial. You will never find peace until you accept that fact. Learn to call on him every day. Tell him you're afraid. Ask for his help. He is with you—and that is enough!

RESPOND

Being mindful of God's presence certainly makes life less frightening, but doing so can be challenging. Here is a simple suggestion. Write down the Lord's message to Joshua on an index card or small piece of paper, adding your name to the verse. For example:

> Be strong and of good courage; be not frightened,
> neither be dismayed, *Gary*; for the Lord your God
> is with you wherever you go.

Now, place the verse in a prominent place such as your office, your car, or the bathroom mirror. Every time you look at it, you will be reminded of something critically important: God is with you!

PRAY

Thank you for always being with me, Lord. Help me to remember your constant presence. Amen.

Day 35

MAKE TIME FOR PRAYER

Tuesday—Fifth Week of Lent

READ

> But [Jesus] withdrew to the wilderness and prayed.
>
> —Luke 5:16

REFLECT

Jesus prayed. While it's hardly a news flash, most of us don't take the time to ponder just how profound of a statement that is. The ultimate goal of Lent (and life) is to imitate Christ. In order to do so, it's important to understand his actions and the reason behind them. Prayer was important to the Lord, so it's a good place to start. Today, let's focus on the three key words from this verse: *withdrew*, *wilderness*, and *prayed*.

The fact that Jesus withdrew implies that it was a conscious decision. His desire to pray was not accidental. Just like each of us, the Lord had to make a choice—to pray or to do something else. How many times do you struggle to fit prayer into your busy life? After all, there are just so many hours in the day. It took me many years to get to this point, but now I wouldn't think of letting a day go by without praying. It's how I begin each day, whether I feel like it or not. Jesus knew that prayer was not so much an action but a relationship.

We live in a noisy world and face many more distractions than the inhabitants of Palestine during the time of Christ. Nonetheless, Jesus made it a point to pray in the wilderness. Why? Because it was quiet and more conducive to having a conversation with his Father. Try to imagine having an intimate conversation with your spouse while the TV is blaring in the background. It just won't work. If you expect to have a conversation with God, you must find a quiet place.

Jesus prayed. That's great, but what exactly is prayer? According to St. Thérèse of Lisieux, "Prayer is a surge of the heart; it is a simple look turned toward heaven, it is a cry of recognition and of love, embracing both trial and joy" (*CCC*, 2558).

We often think of prayer as requesting things from God, but it is so much more. Prayer is a relationship. It is the way we communicate with and relate to our loving Father, through the Son, with the help of the Holy Spirit. Without it, our relationship will wither and die. If you're feeling burned out or worried, there is a good chance that your prayer life is deficient. Look to Jesus as an example and you'll never be led astray.

RESPOND

How is your prayer life? Where is your wilderness? Go to a quiet place (close your office door, take a walk, or get in your car) and spend some time meditating on the prayer life of Jesus. Look for ways that you can pray as he did. Ask the Holy Spirit to point out practices in your life that may need improvement.

PRAY

Jesus, increase my desire to pray as you prayed. Amen.

Day 36

SUFFERING IS A BLESSING

Wednesday—Fifth Week of Lent

READ

> Now I rejoice in my sufferings for your sake, and in my flesh I complete what is lacking in Christ's afflictions for the sake of his body, that is, the church.
>
> —Colossians 1:24

REFLECT

While there are many different reasons for worrying, all of them share a common theme—a fear of suffering. We worry because we are afraid we will have to suffer and we would rather not. It's understandable. Suffering is not fun. And while I want this book to be a source of comfort for you, I must be honest about something. Suffering is unavoidable. We will all go through it at one time or another. The good news is that your pain does not have to be wasted. Suffering can bear great fruit and unite you intimately with Jesus, but you must be willing to use it.

As I write this, there are some especially difficult challenges that I'm facing. Although I know that the Lord is with me, I'm not feeling his presence. Knowing that he can do all things isn't keeping me from feeling a sense of hopelessness. And even though I have asked him to "make everything better," it hasn't happened. I didn't ask for this and I don't really want it, but my suffering gives me the opportunity to help Jesus in his mission of redemption. Confused? The opening verse from St. Paul holds the key.

Although he didn't have to do so, Jesus wants to include us in his redeeming work. As members of his Mystical Body (the Church), we are granted this amazing privilege by Christ himself. Human beings have a natural aversion to suffering, but we can't deny that our redemption took place through the agonizing death of Jesus on the Cross. By uniting our suffering with his, we are able to share in the redemption of all mankind. It's no wonder that Paul was able to rejoice in his intense suffering!

Suffering is a part of life. Sooner or later it's something that we all must face. And, while it's perfectly acceptable to pray that it will be taken away (after all, that's what Jesus did in the Garden of Gethsemane), don't make the mistake of suffering in vain. The life of Christ was filled with humiliation and pain. When you suffer, he is offering you a chance to draw close and share in his pain. It truly is a blessing. Don't waste the opportunity.

RESPOND

Are you suffering now? I invite you to pray the following prayer and give it over to Jesus. It doesn't matter if you feel like doing it. What matters is that you just do it. All of your problems are temporary. They will vanish once you die, or maybe sooner. Offer them up while you still have them.

PRAY

Jesus, I offer up my suffering and unite it with yours. Thank you for the privilege of helping you to redeem the world. Amen.

Day 37

DO YOU BELIEVE?

Thursday—Fifth Week of Lent

READ

> He considered that God was able to raise men even from the dead.
>
> —Hebrews 11:19

REFLECT

At the age of seventy-five, Abraham was asked by God to leave his homeland. He was also told that he would have many descendants—and yet, he would have to wait twenty-five years for that prophesy to be fulfilled. After patiently waiting on the Lord, Abraham saw God's promise fulfilled in Isaac, who was born to Abraham and Sarah when Abraham was one hundred years old (see Genesis 21:1–7).

Several years later, Abraham was asked by God to sacrifice his only son, the source of the promised descendants. Although the Lord prevented him from carrying out the act, Abraham was willing to do it. Was he delusional or some sort of fanatic? Not at all. As this verse tells us, he did it because he trusted God. Abraham knew that the Lord was good for his word and would somehow work out the details. He was right.

Before you feel defeated and believe you'll never be able to have faith like that, here is something you need to remember.

Abraham's faith wasn't always this strong. It grew stronger over the years as he walked with the Lord. Sure, he was able to take that initial leap when he first left his homeland, but there were plenty of slipups along the way. Every time he fell, however, he refocused on the Lord and tried again. Eventually he got to the point of being able to trust radically, knowing that God would not let him down. We may never be able to get to Abraham's level of trust, but that shouldn't stop us from trying. Any growth at all, no matter how small, is a good thing.

Are you struggling to trust the Lord? Have you been crying out to him and not seeing the fruits of your prayers? I'm right there with you and I feel your pain. Let's not forget, however, that it took God twenty-five years to make good on his promise to Abraham. Repeated pleading resulted in the response of "Trust me. It will happen." Eventually, the Lord delivered. Do you wish you had faith like Abraham? It begins by giving God the benefit of the doubt. Are you willing to trust him?

RESPOND

Are you waiting on the Lord to answer a certain prayer right now? You have a great opportunity right before your eyes. Like Abraham, you have a chance to trust God. Doing so will put you on the road to greater faith. Tell the Lord that you trust him even though you're still waiting. Praying like that is a game changer. Just look at Abraham.

PRAY

Dear Lord, I desire to have a stronger faith. Like Abraham, I have made the decision to trust you. It's not easy, but I know that you love me and want what is best in my life. Amen.

Day 38

FIRST THINGS FIRST

Friday—Fifth Week of Lent

READ

> And [Jesus] said to his disciples, "Therefore
> I tell you, do not be anxious about your life,
> what you shall eat, nor about your body,
> what you shall put on."
>
> —Luke 12:22

REFLECT

Case closed, right? We would have to work very hard to interpret this verse in a way that would justify the act of worrying. Jesus is very clear when he tells us that we should not worry, especially about material things. So why do we ignore his words and worry about the things that are temporary? I don't think it's intentional. We often get so caught up in the messiness of life that we lose sight of what really matters. That which is unseen gets eclipsed by what can be seen. Is there anything we can do to correct it?

The first step is to place this verse in its proper context. As Jesus was teaching, someone in the crowd stepped forward with an unusual request: "Teacher, bid my brother divide the inheritance with me" (Lk 12:13).

It was an odd request, considering the fact that Jesus was discussing many things at that time but didn't say a word about money. It's actually a profound insight into the way we think and how often we dwell on material things. In response to this request, Jesus went on to tell the parable of the rich fool (see Luke 12:16–21), a man who found his security in material possessions.

Unfortunately for the rich fool, he neglected the pursuit of spiritual riches and was not in a good place when he died unexpectedly. The moral of the story is that material things should not be our main source of happiness, nor should they be a source of anxiety.

How can we avoid getting caught up in the trap of materialism? Jesus gives us a clue with the words immediately following the verse at the top of this page. He reminds us that life is more than food or clothing. At the same time, he doesn't try to deny that we all have material needs. Rather, he urges us to trust that our heavenly Father will provide us with what we need. While there is certainly a need to do our share (such as looking for work and saving money), our main focus in life should be getting to heaven. Not only will that result in greater peace but also it will put us on the road to eternal happiness.

RESPOND

Take a look at your current prayer intentions and observe how many of them are material in nature. How about spiritual favors? Do you pray for the grace to forgive, to become more patient, or to have greater trust in the Lord? Make a conscious effort to add a few of these spiritual needs to your prayer list.

By doing so, you'll be on your way to doing exactly what the Lord wants.

PRAY

Dear Jesus, in addition to my material needs, please grant me all of the graces necessary to grow closer to you. Amen.

Day 39

THE POWER OF BEING STILL

Saturday—Fifth Week of Lent

READ

Be still, and know that I am God.

—Psalm 46:10

REFLECT

There is a wealth of information in this short verse. Anyone seeking peace will especially benefit from this message. Unfortunately for many of us, it contains a command to do something extremely difficult: be still. In today's fast-paced world, being still is frowned upon as a waste of time. If we want to encounter the Lord and be filled with his peace, however, we must learn to slow down. For it is in these quiet moments that we'll be most receptive to what he has to offer.

There is a good reason that my spiritual director told me that I shouldn't be afraid to "waste" time with the Lord. I have a tendency to approach my spiritual journey as an intellectual pursuit. When I read the Bible, for instance, I push myself to read as much as I can in one sitting. The *Catechism* and other spiritual books are generally read in the same manner. Along the way, I wear out many highlighters and fill up the margins with notes. If I'm going to learn about the Lord, I want to be busy.

The same applies to my prayer life; I typically prefer to do most of the talking. While there's nothing wrong with taking an active role in our pursuit of God, there has to be more. At some point I have to close the books and "waste" time with him. Since he's a participant in our relationship, I have to let him do some of the work. That allows me to know him and not just know *about* him.

Being still also allows me to focus on the other half of this verse—to know that he is God. Unless I meditate on this important truth, I'll never be able to pray with confidence. Concentrating on his identity helps me to remember that I have a best friend who loves me, can fix any problem I encounter, and is with me always. It's a lot easier to be peaceful when we keep these facts in mind. Slow down and think about it. Your outlook will get a whole lot brighter.

RESPOND

Today's response is simple, but it may prove challenging. At some point today (preferably right after you read this), pray the following prayer, close the book, and spend ten minutes in silence with the Lord. Fight the urge to do all of the talking. It may require work, but the end result will be worth it.

PRAY

Lord, help me to be still and to better understand the power of your divinity. Thank you for caring about me. Amen.

Day 40

PALM SUNDAY

THOUGHT FOR THE DAY

My child, know that the greatest obstacles to holiness are discouragement and an exaggerated anxiety. These will deprive you of the ability to practice virtue.

All temptations united together ought not disturb your interior peace, not even momentarily. Sensitiveness and discouragement are the fruits of self-love.

—Jesus to St. Faustina[9]

Day 40

HELP IS ON THE WAY

Palm Sunday

READ

> And as they led him away, they seized one
> Simon of Cyrene, who was coming in from
> the country, and laid on him the cross, to
> carry it behind Jesus.
>
> —Luke 23:26

REFLECT

Today is Palm Sunday, and the fortieth day on our quest to
give up worry. And yet, we have a week to go until this Lenten
journey gives way to Easter joy, so hang in there with me for
just a few more days. After all, giving up worry for Lent isn't
a destination but something that we all need to practice each
day for the rest of our lives, right?

Today at Mass, our attention will be drawn to the Passion
of Jesus Christ. It's a place many of us would rather not go,
but it is somewhere we *must* go. We must go there and join
our sufferings with his so that even our sufferings might be
redeemed. Suffering is part of life. But, as Jesus showed us, it
can also bear great fruit if we understand the value of redemptive suffering, and not give in to despair.

When everything looks dark, it can be hard to get out of bed in the morning. That's why I thought today would be a good day to focus on something that happened on the way to Calvary. In order for Jesus to fulfill his Father's will and die on the Cross, he needed to get there first. After being beaten mercilessly and losing a great deal of blood, it would have been impossible for Jesus to carry the Cross to the place of his death without some assistance. Enter Simon of Cyrene . . .

Simon reminds us that, even during the darkest moments of our lives, God will provide. I'm sure you've heard it before, but do you believe it? As we reflect on the Lord's Passion, let's not overlook the role of the man who just happened to be in the right place at the right time. Although he would probably disagree, Simon of Cyrene was exactly where he needed to be as Jesus made his way to Calvary. While I can't say for sure what may have happened without Simon, I do know what did happen. Simon of Cyrene helped Jesus to carry the Cross to Calvary so that he could die for our sins. God did provide.

Are you struggling to carry your cross? I can say with total confidence that the Lord will assist you. He never gives us crosses that are too heavy to carry. We sometimes feel that way because we forget to ask for help. That help may come in the form of grace or it may come from a Simon of Cyrene—a hospital nurse, a priest, a good friend, a person in the supermarket. These helpers come in all shapes and sizes. Look for your Simon. If he's not here yet, pray for him to arrive. He will be there soon.

RESPOND

Identify the two greatest sources of stress in your life right now. Is there anyone who can help you in any way? Maybe you have a friend who can offer advice or who will roll up the old shirt sleeves and pitch in! Perhaps someone could just lend an ear or give you a shoulder to cry on. Ask the Holy Spirit to bring some names to mind. If you can't think of anyone, maybe the Lord wants to be your Simon. In either case, the next step is the same. Ask for help!

PRAY

Lord, please grant me the help I need to deal with my problems. Amen.

Days 41–47

HOLY WEEK

THOUGHT FOR THE WEEK

Let nothing disturb you,
Let nothing frighten you,
All things are passing away:
God never changes.
Patience obtains all things.
Whoever has God lacks nothing;
God alone suffices.

—St. Teresa of Avila[10]

Day 41

WHY WORRY WHEN YOU CAN PRAY?

Monday of Holy Week

READ

> Have no anxiety about anything, but in
> everything by prayer and supplication with
> thanksgiving let your requests be made
> known to God. And the peace of God,
> which passes all understanding, will keep
> your hearts and your minds in Christ Jesus.
> —Philippians 4:6–7

REFLECT

If you struggle with anxiety, there is a good chance that you
are familiar with this passage of the Bible. In these two verses
are contained a summary of this entire book. Taking it a step
further, this passage provides a daily plan of action for every
Christian. As an added bonus, it gives us an idea of the comfort that we'll experience if we follow these steps.

What I like most about St. Paul's advice is the fact that he's
not just telling us that we shouldn't worry. He is recommend-
ing an alternative action, something that actually does some
good. Unlike the useless act of worry, prayer always yields

results. We may not like the results, but that's another story. Always remember that when you pray, the Lord will respond in some way. Recognizing that we sometimes need to "see" the results of our prayer, however, Paul was inspired to offer some additional incentive. It may be fleeting and it may be subtle, but one of the first fruits of prayer is peace. When we pray, we tend to feel better. That's not an accident. It is a confirmation of this scriptural message. Prayer really works!

As we discussed earlier, St. Paul wrote these words while sitting in a Roman prison. The fact that he could be at peace under those circumstances should give you hope. If he could be peaceful, so can you. The peace offered by Christ isn't dependent on the absence of conflict. To be honest, great suffering often intensifies the peace offered by the Lord. I know it sounds like a paradox, but it is true. I've been there, and I know that Paul's advice works. As the old adage goes, "You'll never know until you try." Do it today. The only thing you have to lose is your anxiety.

RESPOND

All of the suggestions I make in this book have one thing in common—God does most of the work. In this case, our job is to present our needs to the Lord and thank him for responding. The asking part is easy, right? We can all handle that. Thanking him in advance, however, may prove to be a challenge. What if he doesn't answer? Even though we can't be sure how he will respond, we know with certainty that the Lord will respond to our requests. That is reason enough to thank him. Once you do your part, let him do his part. The peace that passes all understanding will be headed your way. How can you refuse an offer like that?

PRAY

Lord, I present all of my problems to you. Thank you for hearing and answering my prayer. Amen.

Day 42

DON'T BE AFRAID TO ASK . . . AND ASK AGAIN!

Tuesday of Holy Week

READ

> So, leaving them again, he went away and prayed for the third time, saying the same words.
>
> —Matthew 26:44

REFLECT

If a close friend approached you and asked for a favor, you would probably do your best to help. How about if your friend came back the next day and made the same request? It still might not be a big deal, but how about if that person came back for the third, fourth, and fifth day in a row, asking for the same thing? You might get annoyed. Most people would.

On the night before he died, Jesus taught us a very important lesson as he addressed his Father in prayer. God doesn't act like most people. If we need something, he wants us to ask, and ask, and ask again.

It doesn't feel right; does it? After all, our heavenly Father is busy and you don't want to bother him. If you keep asking for the same thing over and over, you're only going to annoy him, right? Wrong! Our Father in heaven wants you to depend on him and never tires of your requests. While it's true that all of your prayers shouldn't focus on what you need, prayers of petition are very important. Equally important is the need to be persistent when you pray. If you feel you need something, follow the example of Jesus and keep asking!

You may wonder when it's time to stop praying for a particular intention. Jesus prayed three times using the same words. St. Paul also asked the Lord three times to take away his thorn in the flesh (see 2 Corinthians 12:8). Is three the magic number? While these are definitely two great examples for us to imitate, there is something they have in common that has nothing to do with the number. Both Jesus and Paul prayed until they got an answer. Paul received a no and the promise of grace, while Jesus was sent an angel to strengthen him (see Luke 22:43). We should always continue to pray until the Lord responds with a definitive yes or no.

If you need additional encouragement, consider the following quote from St. Thomas Aquinas. He reminds us that praying for our needs serves an important purpose. "We need to pray to God, not in order to make known to him our needs or desires but that we ourselves may be reminded of the necessity of having recourse to God's help in these matters." [11]

RESPOND

Have you given up praying for a certain intention? If you still feel it's something you need, begin praying for it again. Are you growing weary of praying for something to change in your life? Keep on praying. As we've discussed, praying for the same thing using the same words will not cause God to get annoyed. He is a loving Father who desires that we turn to him for all of our needs.

PRAY

Dear Father, thank you for never getting tired of hearing my prayers. I have many needs, and I know that only you can provide them. Please help me. Amen.

Day 43

WHAT ARE YOU LOOKING FOR?

Wednesday of Holy Week

READ

> As a deer longs
>   for flowing streams,
> so longs my soul
>   for you, O God.
> —Psalm 42:1, RSV:2CE

REFLECT

What were you looking for when you decided to pick up this book? I would expect that "peace" would be the most popular answer. You may have worded it differently (desire to stop worrying, freedom from anxiety, etc.), but the overall goal is the same. Would you be surprised to learn that your desire for peace is actually a quest for something much larger? When we seek peace, we are in reality seeking God. It's such a basic need that we often don't realize it. As our relationship with the Lord grows, so does our peace.

As I mentioned previously, I have looked for peace in many places and things. The world offers a myriad of solutions to those of us seeking freedom from anxiety. Many of them involve distraction, and some are even sinful. Ultimately, they all fall short of the goal. You can only distract yourself or deaden the pain for so long. Unless God is involved, these solutions are temporary. It took me a long time to get this through my thick head, but it is absolutely true.

The fact that you are reading a spiritual book on over-coming worry is a sign that you're on the right track. You may feel as though you're light years away from your destination, but you're not in bad shape. Lots of people never make the connection between God and peace. Understanding that basic concept is a huge accomplishment. If you are seeking the Lord, you will find him. It may take time, but you will eventually succeed. Continue to walk the walk for the remaining few days of Lent. You will eventually find that flowing stream of peace that only the Lord can provide.

RESPOND

How do you seek peace in your life? I know you're reading this book (and that's good), but look at the other ways you seek comfort. Are you trying to replace the Lord's supernat-ural peace with cheap substitutes? Even non-sinful forms of entertainment can sometimes be used as a substitute for God. Spend some time praying about it today. You may discover that you're seeking too much comfort through music and social media. If so, make use of the remaining days of Lent to make some changes.

PRAY

Dear Lord, increase my awareness of the ways that I seek com-fort in the things of this world. Grant me the desire to seek peace in you alone. Amen.

Day 44

THIS IS HOW MUCH JESUS LOVES YOU

Holy Thursday

READ

> And he took bread, and when he had given thanks he broke it and gave it to them, saying, "This is my body which is given for you. Do this in remembrance of me."
>
> —Luke 22:19

REFLECT

In his encyclical on Eucharist in the Church, which was released on Holy Thursday in 2003, St. John Paul II observed:

> The Church draws her life from the Eucharist. This truth does not simply express a daily experience of faith, but recapitulates *the heart of the mystery of the Church*. In a variety of ways she joyfully experiences the constant fulfilment of the promise: "Lo, I am with you always, to the close of the age" (Mt 28:20), but in the Holy Eucharist, through the changing of bread and wine into the body and blood of the Lord, she rejoices in this presence with unique intensity. Ever since Pentecost, when the Church, the People of the New

> Covenant, began her pilgrim journey towards
> her heavenly homeland, the Divine Sacrament
> has continued to mark the passing of her days,
> filling them with confident hope. [12]

There are many ways the Lord could have chosen to accompany us in life. He could have left us an extensive set of writings or merely given us a spiritual presence, but he wanted to do more. By instituting the Sacrament of the Eucharist, Jesus became present to us in the fullest way possible. Under the form of ordinary bread and wine, Jesus Christ appears every day in churches throughout the world. What a blessing! Through the Sacrament of the Eucharist, Christ's Body and Blood are present to us together with his soul and divinity. It's not a symbol or a spiritual presence. It's really him.

Jesus knew how easy it would be to forget about his spiritual presence. We do it several times each day, especially when we get blindsided by unexpected challenges. Therefore, he made himself fully present in this great sacrament. The same Jesus who walked the earth two thousand years ago is available to us every day. If you want to grow close to him, I suggest you begin by receiving the Eucharist as often as possible. You may not feel any different immediately, but something will happen over time. If you are open to receiving the graces that the Lord offers, you will not remain the same.

RESPOND

Are you feeling hopeless? Take a minute to reread what St. John Paul II wrote about the Eucharist in the excerpt from his encyclical. The last line says it all. Frequent reception of

Holy Communion will fill you with "confident hope." If possible, try to receive the sacrament more frequently. Aside from Sunday, see if you can find the time to receive the Lord one or two times during the week. Doing so will make a difference in your life. Even though external circumstances may not change, don't be surprised if your hopelessness gradually changes to hopefulness. The Eucharist is truly that powerful!

PRAY

Dear Jesus, thank you for being present to me in the Eucharist. Please allow me to receive all the graces available in the sacrament. Amen.

Day 45

IT WILL GET BETTER

Good Friday

READ

> I consider that the sufferings of this present time are not worth comparing with the glory that is to be revealed to us.
>
> —Romans 8:18

REFLECT

When I begin to get beaten down by the struggles of life, this is my go-to verse. This message reminds me that this life is temporary. More importantly, it reassures me that the life Christ has planned for me in heaven provides all the happiness I can imagine and then some. It's so good, in fact, that St. Paul instructs us not even to compare it with what we now experience. Today, as we focus the death of Jesus on Calvary, this verse takes on a whole new meaning. Even though it may seem paradoxical, true joy can only be found by picking up our own crosses and following Jesus wherever he chooses to lead.

As difficult as it is to understand why we have to suffer, it's even more difficult to understand why Jesus had to suffer. He did nothing wrong! Couldn't there have been an easier way? In a word, yes! God could have brought about our redemption in any number of painless ways, but he chose to do it this way. As evidenced by Jesus' example, suffering can be beneficial. And as much as I'd like to run away from suffering, how could I claim to be a follower of Christ and be unwilling to follow in his footsteps?

Are you suffering now? This may not make you feel better, but I will say it anyway: *Jesus is calling you to draw near to him.* He wants you to run into his arms and let him comfort you. It's very hard to see suffering as a gift, but that's what it is. Suffering gives us the opportunity to grow close to the Lord and share in his redemptive mission. He always meets us in our suffering. The difficulties you are facing will not last forever, but eternal happiness in heaven will. Jesus loves you so much that he would do anything to allow you to live with him there—even if it meant suffering an agonizing death on the Cross.

RESPOND

On this sad day, Christians around the world mourn the Passion and Death of Jesus Christ. Because of his sacrifice, the gates of heaven were opened to sinners such as you and me. It would be misleading to downplay the physical and emotional suffering that the Lord endured. The pain he felt was very real. And while we should spend time today focusing on his suffering and sacrifice, we don't want to lose sight of the big picture. By pushing through the pain and refusing to come down off the Cross, Jesus accomplished what he set out to do. You have the chance to imitate him and do the same, knowing that he will give you the strength you need.

PRAY

Dear Jesus, thank you for dying on the Cross for me. I offer up all my suffering and unite it with yours. Please grant me the grace to follow through on my promise. Amen.

Day 46

AND SO WE WAIT . . .

Holy Saturday

READ

> Weeping may last for the night,
>   but joy comes with the morning.
> —Psalm 30:5, RSV:2CE

REFLECT

Waiting for medical test results has always been difficult for me. Being a hypochondriac by nature, my mind naturally gravitates toward the worst-case scenario. Although I have been through this drill many times, one case stands out as being especially painful.

After I had been experiencing abdominal discomfort for a period of time, my doctor sent me for a CAT scan. As I typically did, I immediately began waiting for the urgent phone call indicating that there was a serious problem. Two days passed and still no call. I began to hope that maybe all was well. The next day I called my mother to check on her, and after hanging up, I picked up the receiver again to check for messages.

There was a message. Could it be from the doctor? I entered the code, and my suspicion was correct! My heart began to race as my doctor indicated that the test results were in. He then proceeded to tell me two things that I didn't want to hear: (1) he was leaving for the night, and (2) he wanted me to come in and see him the next day.

As you might imagine, I got very little sleep that night as I assumed the worst. Why would he want to see me unless the test had revealed something very, very serious?

Ultimately, all of this ended up being no big deal. The doctor just wanted to let me know that the scan raised some questions and some additional testing was recommended. He was not concerned, and the tests ended up confirming his belief. I wish he had told me that when he left the message, as it would have saved me a great deal of worrying!

When Jesus died, many of his followers were devastated. They lost hope and were grief stricken, totally forgetting that he had promised to rise from the dead. They didn't need to despair; what they needed to do was wait. In the end, everything would work out just as he had said. It would take three days, but he would rise. I don't know what the future holds for you, but I do know that many of the things that are causing you to lose sleep will turn out fine. Taking a quick look at your worrying history should confirm that for you. We have all wasted a great deal of time worrying about potential problems that never amounted to anything. It's Holy Saturday and the Lord has not yet risen from the dead. No problem. Wait until you see what happens tomorrow!

RESPOND

It took three days for Jesus to rise from the dead. Don't give up on the Lord if he doesn't answer your prayers overnight.

Sometimes he takes his time. Today is a day of waiting. It's a good day to ask for the patience to trust that the Lord's timing is always perfect.

PRAY

Dear Lord, please help me to remain hopeful as I wait for you to act in my life. Amen.

Day 47

JESUS DOESN'T LIE

Easter Sunday

READ

> He is not here; for he has risen, as he said.
> —Matthew 28:6

REFLECT

The Lord is risen! This is such a big deal that the Church will celebrate his Resurrection for the next seven weeks. We rejoice because death has been transformed into the gateway to eternal life. The gates of heaven have been opened by the Lord's Death and Resurrection. This news is so exciting that we sometimes lose sight of another important, but often overlooked, fact. Jesus said he would rise from the dead. Today he made good on that promise.

While rising from the dead is certainly the most important promise that Christ fulfilled, there were many others as well. Let's take a look at a few of his other promises.

- "Behold, I stand at the door and knock; if any one hears my voice and opens the door, I will come in to him and eat with him, and he with me" (Rv 3:20). *Have you opened the door of your heart to Jesus, and invited him in?*

- "And I tell you, Ask, and it will be given you; seek, and you will find; knock, and it will be opened to you" (Lk 11:9). *Is there something you have been asking the Lord for, something that has required persistent effort in prayer on your part?*
- "With men this is impossible, but with God all things are possible" (Mt 19:26). *Have you asked the Lord to stretch your "faith muscles," so that you can trust him more and more?*
- "In the world you have tribulation; but be of good cheer, I have overcome the world" (Jn 16:33). *Have you been practicing thankfulness, even in the dark times of your life?*
- "All things are possible to him who believes" (Mk 9:23). *Have you grown in your ability to trust God for his best for you, rather than your own version of "best"?*
- "Come to me, all who labor and are heavy laden, and I will give you rest" (Mt 11:28). *As you conclude this book and begin to walk with the Lord, have you asked him to carry the burdens for you that are too hard for you to bear alone?*

If Jesus followed through on his promise of rising from the dead, doesn't it make sense that he'll deliver on the other promises as well? Somehow we still manage to doubt; don't we? We look at the difficulties facing us and forget all about his promises of peace, rest, and doing the impossible. Jesus Christ died and rose from the dead. Don't allow yourself to become desensitized. He was dead and now he lives. When was the last time you saw that happen? If he did that, why can't he do the other things he promised?

RESPOND

As we celebrate the Lord's Resurrection, I encourage you to spend a little time looking at some of the other things he promised. Most of our worries revolve around our inability to believe his words. I know it's not easy, but that's why we are given the gift of faith when we are baptized. Through that gift, we are given the ability to believe that what he said is true. Whether we do or not is up to us. Think about the Resurrection and then make your decision. Jesus is a man of his word. Putting your trust in him is a very wise decision.

PRAY

Dear Jesus, thank you for fulfilling your promise to rise from the dead. Please help me to believe your other promises as well. Amen. Alleluia!

Conclusion

"THE BEGINNING"

Congratulations! You have arrived at a new beginning. Seven weeks ago, you left your old way of life and tried something new. Beginning on Ash Wednesday, you heard the Lord speak to you every day through sacred scripture. Some of his words probably seemed more pertinent than others, and that's a good thing. He often surprises us by telling us things that we don't expect to hear. That's the beauty of a personal relationship with Jesus.

As you probably noticed, not all of the verses in this book mentioned anxiety. That was intentional. Even though this book was designed to help you stop worrying, there is an underlying goal that is even more important—your entering into a deep, personal relationship with Jesus Christ. Ultimately, that relationship is what will give you lasting peace. Even better, it will get you to heaven.

After reading this book, I can't promise that you will never worry again. I will tell you that if you continue the practice of meeting the Lord through prayer, scripture, and the sacraments, your level of peace will increase. How much? I can't say exactly, but it is generally directly proportional to the amount of time you spend with him. As I have said before, I am an anxious person by nature. My mind typically gravitates toward to the worst-case scenario. I have a strong tendency to play the "What if?" game. My life changed dramatically when I encountered Jesus and surrendered my life to him. I continue to walk with him every day, and it has made a huge difference. I am very much at peace. You can be too. Jesus is the answer. Stay close to him and you'll see what I mean. Remember that this is a process. Don't give up. Nothing is impossible for God.

I'll be praying for you. Please pray for me, too.

Notes

1. Becky Benante, ed., *In the Heart of the World* (Novato, CA: New World Library, 1997), 17.

2. Fulton J. Sheen, *On Being Human: Reflections on Life and Living* (Garden City, NY: Doubleday, 1982), 36.

3. Second Vatican Council, Dogmatic Constitution on Divine Revelation *Dei Verbum*, November 18, 1965, 21, www.vatican.va.

4. John Paul II, Homily for the Inauguration of His Pontificate, October 22, 1978, 5, www.vatican.va.

5. Raymond Arroyo, ed., *Mother Angelica's Little Book of Life Lessons and Everyday Spirituality* (New York: Doubleday, 2007), 127.

6. Francis, Morning Meditation, "Three Doors," May 16, 2014, www.vatican.va.

7. Anthony Chiffolo, ed., *Padre Pio: In My Own Words* (Liguori, MO: Liguori Publications, 2000), 84.

8. Catherine M. Odell, *Father Solanus Casey* (Huntington, IN: Our Sunday Visitor, 2017), 253.

9. Maria Faustina Kowalska, *Diary of Saint Maria Faustina Kowalska: Divine Mercy in My Soul* (Stockbridge, MA: Marian Press, 1987), 1488.

10. This is an adaptation of Teresa of Avila's prayer, "Efficacy of Patience." The original can be found in *The Collected Works of St. Teresa of Avila*, trans. by Kieran Kavanaugh, O.C.D., vol. 3 (Washington, DC: ICS Publications, 1985), 386.

11. Thomas Aquinas, *Summa Theologiae*, 2.2.83:2.

12. John Paul II, Encyclical *Ecclesia de Eucharistia*, April 17, 2003, 1, www.vatican.va.

GARY ZIMAK serves as director of parish services at Mary, Mother of the Redeemer Catholic Church in North Wales, Pennsylvania. He also is the host of *Spirit in the Morning* on Holy Spirit Radio in Philadelphia. He is a frequent speaker and retreat leader at Catholic parishes and conferences across the country.

Zimak is the author of seven books, including *A Worrier's Guide to the Bible, Listen to Your Blessed Mother, From Fear to Faith*, and *Stop Worrying and Start Living*. His work has appeared in *Catholic Exchange, Catholic Digest*, the *National Catholic Register*, and *Catholic Answers* magazine. He has appeared on numerous television and radio programs, including EWTN's *Bookmark* and *Women of Grace, The Jennifer Fulwiler Show, Catholic Connection, Morning Air*, and the *Son Rise Morning Show*.

Zimak earned a bachelor of science degree in business administration from Drexel University.

He lives in Mount Laurel, New Jersey, with his wife. They have two children.

www.FollowingTheTruth.com
Facebook: Gary.Zimak.speaker.author
Twitter: @gary_zimak

AVE

AVE MARIA PRESS

Founded in 1865, Ave Maria Press,
a ministry of the Congregation of
Holy Cross, is a Catholic publishing
company that serves the spiritual and
formative needs of the Church and its
schools, institutions, and ministers;
Christian individuals and families; and
others seeking spiritual nourishment.

For a complete listing of titles from

Ave Maria Press

Sorin Books

Forest of Peace

Christian Classics

visit www.avemariapress.com

AVE MARIA PRESS
Notre Dame, IN
A Ministry of the United States Province of Holy Cross